· The ·
IMPERIAL
MIDDLE

By Benjamin DeMott

NOVELS

The Body's Cage
A Married Man

CULTURE CRITICISM

Hells & Benefits
You Don't Say
Supergrow
Surviving the Seventies
The Imperial Middle

TEXTBOOKS

America in Literature
Close Imagining

· The ·
IMPERIAL
MIDDLE

*Why Americans Can't
Think Straight
About Class*

·

BENJAMIN DeMOTT

*William Morrow and Company, Inc.
New York*

Library of Congress Cataloging-in-Publication Data

DeMott, Benjamin, 1924–
    The imperial middle : why Americans can't think straight about
class / Benjamin DeMott.
       p. cm.
    Includes bibliographical references
    ISBN 1-55710-023-3
    1. Social classes—United States.   2. Equality—United States.
3. Social conflict—United States.   I. Title.
HN90.S6D46   1990
305.5'0973—dc20   90-34634
                                                    CIP

Printed in the United States of America

2 3 4 5 6 7 8 9 10

BOOK DESIGN BY JAYE ZIMET

To Jo

CONTENTS

INTRODUCTION

*M*y subject is a nation in shackles, its thought, character, and public policy locked in distortion and lies. The deceit I speak of corrodes every aspect of American life. It legitimizes, in war, arrangements exempting without cause large sectors of the younger male population from the burdens and sacrifice of service. It grants giant subsidies for housing, education, and health care in obedience to a single precept: benevolence is most deserved where least needed. It intimates in contempt of reality that whatever injustice exists in America resides on the margins and among the minorities, remote from the center and the majority. And it produces a culture in which men and women of intellectual and artistic talent are persuaded that the highest cause such talent can serve is that of its own independence, and that disdain for the spirit of affiliation and solidarity is among the primary obligations of genius.

Several hallowed concepts—independence, individualism, choice—are woven into this web of illusion and self-deception. But presiding over the whole stands the icon of *classlessness*—the myth asserting, as President George Bush puts it, that class is "for European democracies or something else—it isn't for the United States of America. We are not going to be divided by class." The power of this icon of classlessness derives from history, the media, and the national experience of public education, and much of *The Imperial Middle* probes the interaction of these forces in shaping American social opinion. But the power of the idea of the classless society also stems from tendencies among the educated and sophisticated—the practice of dealing with class in terms either frivolous (classifications of buying habits as "prole," "middle," or "upper") or arcane (squabbles by academic Marxists and post-Marxists about "class instrumentalism," "hegemony," the "ethico-political sphere," and the like).

This book is most emphatically *not* an attempt to anatomize the social differences in our midst. On occasion it examines models of the class system constructed by writers and pollsters. But it does so only as part of a general effort to sort out and compare the basic images, assumptions, and knowledge of class now passing current in the society. Understanding of class differs from class to class. In the community of the educated and sophisticated, class is commonly understood as the inherited accumulation of property, competencies, beliefs, tastes, and manners that determines, for most of us, our socioeconomic lot and our share of civic power. But this very definition is the target of unrelenting fire in the media and in public discourse. And a large body of evidence indicates that the attack upon it, working in concert with other influences analyzed below, is among the forces enabling the state to behave as though episodes of state-administered injustice are accidents, queer events on the fringes, occurrences in no way rooted in the belief system understood as "Americanism." Putting the same point in other terms: *social wrong is accepted in America partly because differences in knowledge about class help to obscure it, and the key to those differences is the degree of acceptance of the myth of classlessness.* This book attempts to lay bare the links between the perpetuation of the myth and the perpetuation of social wrong.

To some minds, inevitably, talk of lies and deception will imply conspiracy—a broadscale, conscious venture in thought control, directed by shrewdly concealed propaganda czars. But in fact no conspiracy exists, none is needed, and the hunt for individual villains only trivializes the problem. Admittedly the temptation to launch a hunt at times becomes severe. Confronted with a huge untruth the human costs of which still remain hidden, the mind longs for clear bills of indictment.

But the longing itself is part of the problem, not the solution, and must be resisted. Doubtless there are scriptwriters, politicos, editorial writers and commentators in number who "know," in some sense, that the versions of the structure of American society they purvey are less than accurate—but none qualifies on that account as a master liar or conspirator. Over time an immense weight of opinion has gathered on the side of social untruth; the means available to those who attempt to contend against the untruth are fragile; the few contenders often fall into self-righteousness, humorlessness, academic convolution, and podium sonority. And, after all, the social untruth at which they joust isn't at every level dysfunctional: it pleases a significant sector of the population, supports a go-ahead, optimistic mentality, and, most important, swells currents of irreverence that undeniably freshen the culture as a whole. Where there is no market for the truth, no evident desire or need for it, and no easy, attractive language in which to frame it (*classless* and *class-lessness* are, as I admit, highly unappetizing terms), truth-telling is hardly a live option. We are closer to fact, in short, when we think of the deceit in which we're locked as a culture-wide consensual evasion rather than as a product of individual, willfully immoral prevaricators.

But it's one thing to acknowledge this and another altogether to blink away the essential truth: America as a classless society is, finally, a deceit, and today, as yesterday, the deceit causes fearful moral and social damage.

The task for this book is to do as much as can be done, in the space of a single work, to clarify the nature of the pressures preventing the society from comprehending its own character and structure. We start with a sampling of American talk—our ways of placing each other socially and our methods of dancing away from consciousness of the implications of those acts of placement. The focus then shifts to the modes of operation, on the American mind, of the dominant influences shaping the mythology of classlessness. (The subjects engaged range from the premises of sitcoms to U.S. labor history, from the evolution of common schooling to the emergence of a new psychological pattern—"the omni syndrome" —in response to demands of the received American social religion.) Attention turns later to resources available to people determined to overcome fantasy—works of social thought, history, and criticism that open paths toward moral and political realism.

Cultural materials of many kinds serve as the ground of analysis—movies, novels, cartoons, sculpture, poems, jokes, statistics, the language of "news," much more. The theme, however, remains constant: the need to bring difference alive, and the possibility of restoring our power to see others feelingly in their separateness and distinctness.

Few noble American dicta are quoted more often than Learned Hand's observations on the "spirit of liberty"—"the spirit which seeks to understand the minds of other men and women," weighing the interests of others alongside their own, "without bias." But even among those who have the passage by heart there's too little realization that the first step toward achieving the spirit of liberty is the development of a capacity to *believe* in difference and to register it, to imagine one's way deeply into the moment-to-moment feelings and attitudes of people placed differently from oneself. The end of the myth of classlessness requires the beginning of awareness that details of feeling, and of knowledge, differ vastly from class to class, and that the differences are not abstract.

The differences are not abstract. Ten years ago, at Amherst College where I teach, a black freshman named Gerald Penny went down the hill to the gym with his classmates, during "orientation," to take a compulsory swimming test. Rows of larking students—mainly children of affluence—dove one after another into the pool, filling the lanes. Penny dove with the others, and, not knowing how to swim, drowned. (The college's Black Cultural Center now bears Penny's name.)

The institution responded earnestly to the lesson the episode taught. It arranged for new safety precautions, sponsored talks. There was no callousness; a theme emphasized in the speeches was that such disasters demonstrate that the "previous experiences of blacks and whites aren't the same." Little time was spent elucidating these differences and the subject of class went unmentioned, but the moment nevertheless dislodged many from their condition of unwitting confinement. A hideous, shaming drowning stimulates the constructive imagination, generating questions that bring difference to truly vivid life. The black lad at poolside becomes a presence in the mind as he stands and waits, thinking to himself (was it in bewilderment or terror? might he have felt anticipation?) that these classmates jumping and diving into the water are enjoying themselves, appear to be in perfect command. Having fun! Should he be mortified by his hesitation? Is he a coward? a baby? Perhaps young Penny decided on the spot that he himself must know how to swim as a matter of basic God-given coordination, and that what happens when a person jumps into the water is that he at once becomes a swimmer by instinct, no problem. . . .

Needless to continue. A defined, tragic, human situation obviously teaches one very swiftly how to begin framing questions that bring difference alive. The point that matters is that a culture so oblivious as to require shocks of this kind before focusing its imagination on difference—and (one may note parenthetically) a culture committed to the notion that class differences count only when race differences enter the equation—probably should not trust itself to deal wisely, by instinct, with what it recognizes as its "social problems," and may well have large problem areas to which it is utterly blind. There is no instant corrective, of course, but there are goals worth pursuing. The first is the banishment of suspicion that realistically weighing class differences, in order to sharpen sensitivity and repair social policy, is in any respect un-American. The second goal is the development of habits of response and thought that are *steadily* alert to the difference class makes. My book will succeed if it contributes to these ends.

· *Part I* ·
VOICES OF
THE MYTH

■

• Chapter 1 •

TALKING ABOUT
EACH OTHER

*I*n theory, class is an unmentionable ("I don't want to get into class," said Senator Dole in Campaign '88, before getting into class); actually it comes up often. A friend explains a third party by mentioning social origins. ("Ken's dad was a big orthopedic surgeon in St. Louis, did you know?" "Susie's an Arkansas gal, did you know? Left for college right off the farm." "Roger's from a Catholic family in Eau Claire. Seven kids and the mother was an RN.") Students or children are overheard using their own class vocabulary—"greaser," "preppie," and the like—to categorize behavior, clothes, and people. Media heroes work class details into their acts, as when a Johnny Carson monologue looks back—and down—on the pastoral mores of Nebraska from the eminence of a Malibu beach house.

Take a random walk any day through the culture, attending to the trivial as well as the weighty, and class regularly turns up. And much of the talk is funny, as in the work of the cartoonists. Week after week these amused eyes focus on the doings of the déclassé (George Price and George Booth) and the elites (William Hamilton, Richard Cline, Jules Feiffer). Cline chuckles at curly-haired yuppies disparaging each other's "personal growth." Hamilton chuckles at hip, power-breakfasting moguls ("Shall we talk ninja to ninja?"). Feiffer passes on the tragedy of Fred who failed to get to Choate. That story is told (in a seven-panel strip) by Fred's dour-featured mom, and it starts with an excoriation of Fred's dad for not pushing "to get Fred into the right schools." Denied "the right education" and "the right contacts," Fred sank fast, it seems. Today he "tends bar, eats tacos and has married a bleached blonde," thereby joining "a class my father slaved a lifetime to raise us above." The coda: "My husband wonders why I left him. The answer is why didn't you send Fred to Choate." From the speaker's bleak, bitter face we learn plenty, obliquely, about Fred's taco-jocund liberation—how it feels to be free at last of contacts-anxiety, Grandpa's legend, and the grousing of a Choate-crazed mom. For those learned in the pertinent social valences it's a pointed bit.

Coarser jokes than Feiffer's are told in corridors—any corridor, school, office, or ward; class jokes with ethnic covers. There was this star and director discussing the new starlet on the set and:

Director: She's Polish.

Star: Polish! Who says?

Director: Gotta be. She's fucking the writer.

Most Polish jokes consist of class insult, ethnically masked, and it's well not to shout when telling some of them. The one, for instance, in Ann Beattie's *Falling in Place* (1980) about why a Polish woman is different from a bowling ball. "If you were really hungry, you could eat a bowling ball."

During football games and other family shows, comic styles change, becoming more physical and featuring a measure of kidding around. John Madden, the former coach, kids around about linemen as "hogs." He's pure empathy, putting his beefy bulk into motion—hands, arms, shoulders, head—re-creating players berserk for the sack hurling themselves into the wall, roaring dementedly (*where is he, gimme an arm, let me at him, smash him, where is the sucker, I'll kill him*). The exuberantly affectionate mimicry softens the content, and the link to tradition is evident. For a century this country has been smiling at clod-athletes—big, slightly dim lads who come off the farm or out of the mines and are destined (says convention) soon to return. Madden loves pro linemen, but he smiles, too. Best to smile, actually, when calling chaps hogs.

At night there's David Letterman, who isn't an empathizer. In teasing man-in-the-street interviews, patches of impatient reading of viewer mail, soliloquies voicing vexation at the service industry work force, the star obliquely derides the working-class world. On one show Letterman runs on at length about his dislike of the fat red hands of a young female cashier at a grocery checkout counter, and the next night he seems to be squirming. He cries out to Paul that he himself was a bagger in youth. An apology of a kind.

Once again there's a softening persona: Letterman is an *anti*-host. Death to fake chumminess, is his motto. Banish grinning, upbeat, commercial, "have-a-nice-day" warmth. Disdain is a mere detail in the broader characterization, which gives us David Letterman as a man so troubled by hype he's forced to become a curmudgeon. And the hype-rejecting persona is further complicated by boyishly nice features that each night smuggle charm onto the show through hidden side doors. But class ridicule seeps almost continuously into the act, and more often than not it's the bottom dog who's the butt of the jokes.

Mass audience jokes they are, not intricate witty tropes.

Like Madden, Polish jokes, and cartoons, David Letterman belongs to the airy world of pop. But high culture—literature and the arts—could easily be included on this random walk. Open any freshman anthology and a great chorus of voices talking class pours forth—among them Elizabeth Bishop's voice, reacting to life at the gas station:

FILLING STATION

Oh, but it is dirty!—
this little filling station,
oil-soaked, oil-permeated
to a disturbing, over-all
black translucency.
Be careful with that match!

Father wears a dirty,
oil-soaked monkey suit
that cuts him under the arms,
and several quick and saucy
and greasy sons assist him
(it's a family filling station)
all quite thoroughly dirty.

Do they live in the station?
It has a cement porch
behind the pumps, and on it
a set of crushed and grease-
impregnated wickerwork;
on the wicker sofa
a dirty dog, quite comfy.

Some comic books provide
the only note of color—
of certain color. They lie
upon a big dim doily
draping a taboret
(part of the set), beside
a big hirsute begonia.

Why the extraneous plant?
Why the taboret?
Why, oh why, the doily?
(Embroidered in daisy stitch
with marguerites, I think,
and heavy with gray crochet.)

Somebody embroidered the doily.
Somebody waters the plant,
or oils it, maybe. Somebody
arranges the rows of cans
so that they softly say:
ESSO-SO-SO-SO
to high-strung automobiles.
Somebody loves us all.

Not all the class talk that surfaces from day to day qualifies as funny. Much of it is appreciative/congratulatory, reflecting enthusiasm and pleasure. And one other, quite different style warrants mention; it's best described as hard-nosed.

Congratulatory class talk involves bestowals of praise on blacks, Asians, Irish, and others who have become worthy of applause from the rest of us. Black quarterbacks, for example, who amaze us by rising from nowhere to star in the Super Bowl, or fellows in the mailroom who, over the years, hang in there uncomplainingly. *The New Yorker* recently printed a tribute to a deserving, deceased layout man named John Murphy, noting that "he considered himself a working man who did his job," "didn't bellyache about whatever the good Lord sent his way," and was "a master at telling the sort of joke associated with salesmen and bartenders." Out in the provinces, today as in Flaubert's time, the congratulatory mode is used in appreciations of cooks, bakers, and quilters. A local paper visits a quilt show and salutes the prizewinners. "The top was done by Laotian refuges (*sic*), and Quida McAliley of Geneva did the quilting. Their hand-work was actually nicer than hers."

Hard-nosed class talk can bring a person up short. I was on a Saturday grocery line, during a summer visit to East Hampton, and the woman in front of me tapped the shoulder of the woman in front of her. "Are you a native?" she asked. The woman addressed said Yes, smiling uncertainly. "Well, tell me something," said the first woman irritably. "Why don't you do your shopping on weekdays?"

Or you're watching *Terms of Endearment* again with your kids and comes a supermarket scene that for some reason you remember. Debra Winger's character discovers, after her groceries are punched up, that she hasn't enough money to pay for them. People are waiting behind her. A debate commences between Debra Winger and her youngster about what to return to the shelves. As mother and son squabble, snatching items from each other, the cashier struggles to re-total—once, twice, three times. The third time she realizes the sum isn't being reduced. "Hey, we're going in the wrong direction." "Why do you have to be so goddamn nasty?" says Debra Winger. A friendly banker behind Debra intervenes, lends her money, and chides the cashier. He calls her "a very rude young woman," and says he knows her boss wouldn't want her "treating customers so badly." The cashier says she doesn't think she was rude. "Then you must be from New York," says the banker, played by John Lithgow. The movie puts us firmly on the banker's side. Not only is he a banker, he's against New York and friendly to the star, whereas the person talking back to him is, after all, a checkout counter girl.

Or you are reading *Vanity Fair*, the magazine. One piece celebrates CBS's Diane Sawyer for her million-plus salary, beauty, education (Wellesley), political connections (Nixon, Kissinger, Holbrooke), embossed Tiffany stationery; the writer concludes Diane is an American classic ("How she *moves!*"). The neighbor piece takes out after Donna Rice, noting her low past (birthplace: Irmo, S. C.; education: State U.; religious affiliation: Southern Baptist), her pushy determination "to use her looks to make the right connections"; terms like "tramp" and "lowlife" are used throughout the article, and the writer concludes that Ms. Rice "does not even qualify as a villain, since she is a character with no center, no concrete goal. . . ."

Here's a TV piece in the morning paper questioning the producer of a sitcom called *Married . . . With Children*. The show is about a shoe store salesman and his wife, who are presented as loud, boorish, and mean to each other. Why these characterizations? asks the reporter. The co-creators explain that "We sat around thinking: does anyone have a family like [Cosby]? Wasn't there a family where the guy had a job that he hated? We couldn't think of anything that would depress a man more [than selling shoes]. There seemed something about kneeling at the foot of a fat woman and trying to wedge her foot into a shoe that was incredibly depressing."

The lead-in to *Married . . . With Children*, on the Fox

channel, is a cartoon show called *The Simpsons*, which presents another working class family: goonlike dad, dim mom, bratty kids.

On the front page of the *Boston Globe* there's news of a labor dispute. The management of the Copley Plaza in Boston is fighting with the chambermaids. Management has promulgated a new rule: forget mops when cleaning bathrooms, scrub on your hands and knees. "There will be no mops used in the rooms of this hotel until further notice! ... Help yourself to as many clean rags as you like for HAND-washing floors." The hotel and restaurant workers union is filing a grievance. Mayor Flynn is canceling the inaugural ball that was scheduled for the Copley Plaza. The paper says the mayor's mother was a chambermaid. The paper also says that the management of the Ritz-Carlton has no anti-mops rule.

A maid who asks that her name not be used tells a reporter she finds the no-mops rule "downgrading" to her. The leader of the hotel workers union asks the public to imagine a concrete situation: "the scene of a white male sitting in his hotel reading *The Wall Street Journal* while the black maid is in the bathroom on her hands and knees." Alan Tremain, president of the firm that operates the hotel, defends the anti-mops rule: "I don't see it as a hardship," he insists. "A maid is a maid and this is just what she has to do."

Our random walk is only starting. There are ads to look at. Campaign managers talking about constituencies (blue-collar, Joe Sixpack, Chablis and Volvo set, etc.). There are soaps, cop shows, and fashion magazines, the art of Robert De Niro, videos of Michael Jackson, club bulletins, general conversation, college catalogs ... But no need just now for a deluge of detail. The point is simply that class does come up a lot, and a portion of the talk seems harsh. A maid is a maid, athletes are hogs, checkout girls are ugly, checkout girls are mean, shoe salesmen are boorish, bartenders are slobs, gas station attendants are filthy, poor pretty ambitious girls are tarts, rich pretty accomplished girls are saints. . . .

When account is taken of the self-concepts of the speakers, it immediately becomes clear that few of them understand themselves to be talking class—or to be talking harshly. To Alan Tremain, the hotel spokesman, "a maid is a maid" means something like: *People are so damned dim about the facts of the work world. Nobody understands anything. Hardship! Hey, when you start down that ladder, you soon get to a place where a job is a simple set of physical operations the boss tells you to do. That's it. People on the scene know this. They know the difference between a busboy and an assistant night manager. If these reporters would wake up, they'd get it, too. They'd realize changes in job specs come with the territory. They don't mean diddley splat to staff.*

"A maid is a maid," in short, isn't felt as an expression of a class-specific attitude and isn't meant to wound. The speaker imagines himself to be communicating plain unvarnished truths of the workplace.

Nor does the local paper feel itself to be looking down as it announces its surprise that the handwork of Laotians might beat that of Quida McAliley. The remark fuses tolerance and self-esteem. *We give credit where credit is due. These dreadfully poor people haven't a thing. They're dependents! But will you look at that needlework? People ought to remember this when they go around thinking inhospitable thoughts about strangers in our midst.*

Madden and Letterman are entertainers, and as such, win the standard jesters' exemption from earnest scrutiny. The article writers in *Vanity Fair* are, in their self-conception,

moralists not classists. Donna Rice behaved *badly*, lived with
a man later convicted of dope dealing, spent a night with
another woman's husband. Diane Sawyer is forty-one; she
married late, lives for her career. In the mind of the article
writer it's moral indignation, not class prejudice, that puts
Donna down and Diane up.

And as for Elizabeth Bishop the poet, bemused by the
greasy family that oils its plants instead of watering them:
class enters her poem but so, too, does the mystery of grace.
"Filling Station" registers the truth that huge dissimilarities
exist within the human family; some people are gorgeously
attractive, others make the gorge rise. Most love themselves,
or love each other, and yet the Creator must somehow love
them all, the Diane Sawyers and the greasers. Love therefore
is the subject, and class is the screen.

This sense of class as screen—this readiness at once to
embrace and reject class talk, this having-it-both-ways style
of allusion to social difference—helps to illuminate the nature
of the problem. It tells us, quite simply, that the problem is
not at bottom one of ill will. Granted, the attitudes expressed
come across frequently as repellent and hurtful. A maid is a
maid, a man is a hog, checkout girls' hands are disgusting. . . .
These ways of speaking hardly foster fraternal feeling.

But the subtler and deeper significance of American class
talk reaches far beyond personal relationships, extending to
public policy and the basic situation of the state. By talking
class while denying explicitly or implicitly that class is meant,
speakers cope with a central national paradox, namely that
they belong to a class society that is nevertheless highly gra-
tified by its egalitarian ideals. The practice of coping in this
fashion with paradox—treating it with light irony and the
cartoonist's detachment, instead of confronting it for what it

is: a major source of confusion and inequity in every sector from schooling to tax-supported retirement—permits leaders and followers alike to avoid fundamental questions. Does the assertion that there are no classes in America carry with it an assurance that legislative and administrative instruments actually behave as though the populace were classless? If so, does such behavior on the part of the state truly serve the interests of fairness? And if these and related questions are too complex in their ramifications to permit blunt affirmative or negative answers, can evidence be cited establishing that the state is alert to the complexities—takes reasonable account of them when setting policy?

The gap between Polish jokes and queries on this scale is clearly immense; closing it requires attention to many subjects that seldom figure in discussions of the shaping of public policy. And the pursuit of those subjects, which include both the moral and social assumptions and the cultural and historical forces that nourish the concept of classless class, cannot be conducted without immersion in several modes of American evasion, contradiction, and fantasy. It bears reiterating here, therefore, that the purpose of the pursuit is not that of laughing at self-delusion; it is to provide a groundwork for clarification of the principal conditions of this country's political and intellectual life.

- *Chapter 2* -

CLASS DISMISSED

Class is a ripoff run by prestige-peddlers.
Class is temporary and various.
Class is a mask that genial good sense sees through.

*T*he assumptions brought together in the mythology of classlessness perform a number of complementary functions. They supply terms of disparagement applicable to those who treat class straightforwardly as a matter of high seriousness. They outline—vaguely yet seductively—grounds for discounting the evident social differences in our midst. And by indirection they account for the presumed American uniqueness—our imagined luck in escaping the hierarchies that burden the rest of the developed world. Some of the assumptions in question center on the nature and meaning of class itself; others on the special character of the American populace, viewed in social terms; all without exception are interdependent.

1. *Class is a ripoff run by prestige-peddlers.*

In the Eighties two quite widely read treatises on class appeared in England and America—Jilly Cooper's *Class* (1981) and Paul Fussell's *Class* (1983). Both works amusingly describe class differences as represented in dress, styles of consumption, verbal and sexual behavior, other manners. Both works come to decisions about how many classes in the respective homelands warrant separate labeling. (Cooper decides English society has six separate classes; Fussell argues America has nine.)

Here the similarities end. Cooper, the Englishwoman, begins her book with an extended account of her own social location within the middle class—two full pages of concrete detail on subjects ranging from the occupations and religious backgrounds of the previous three to four generations of her family to the landholdings (seven acres) and style of architecture (Georgian) of the house she grew up in. Thereafter she alludes constantly both to this specific class identity and to the likelihood that as she places others in daily life, at parties and elsewhere (above, below, one of us), they in turn are placing her. ("... Quite often you think you are being terribly democratic talking to some vulgar little man at a party, while he at the same time is thinking how decent he is wasting time on someone as socially insignificant as you.") On occasion, Cooper's own children enter the act: "I once heard my son regaling his friends: 'Mummy says "pardon" is a much worse word than "fuck". ' " The impression is of a sensibility ceaselessly conscious of the dynamics of class encounter, aware both of differences in consumer choices and of exclusions and barriers facing citizens "if [they] come from a particular class," and entangled at each moment in social coils from which extrication is finally perceived as neither conceivable nor desirable.

Paul Fussell, the American, begins his book not by defining his personal place in a hierarchy but with a general discussion of society as a whole, special emphasis on the delusions of status-obsessed consumers of cars, houses, furniture, art, drinks, schools, hairstyles, and so on. Nowhere is he seen caught in a web of class identities and definitions, feeling the pressure of being categorized as he categorizes. His role is that of a cataloguer of self-deceptions and vanities among "upper middles," "middles," and "proles" who share the dimwitted notion that true distinction can be bought. "If the living rooms of the top classes tend to ape art galleries and museums," he writes, "those of the middle class and below resemble motel rooms. Socially crucial is the dividing line where original works of art or *virtu* are replaced by reproductions. The Tiffany lamp is a case in point. It lost caste fatally the moment reproductions with plastic 'glass' began showing up in middle-class houses and restaurants, and now one sees the things even in prole settings."

Fussell is male, Cooper female; the strength of the autobiographical impulse varies from writer to writer; audience expectations influence writers' perspectives. (The need for an enlivening personal perspective increases when subjects are perceived as worn, and English audiences surely perceive the subject of class as worn.) But the chief difference between these two writers lies in the respect they accord to class. Both find humor in the subject, but the American's humor rides on contempt. Jilly Cooper holds that class decisively conditions each individual human being, herself included, throughout the life cycle; not an entirely salutary force, it's no put-on, either. Class-based responses seem as natural to her as breathing and eating; one *is*, she assumes, one's class. Whereas Paul Fussell strongly implies that he himself is classless, that class is an option not a fate (an option taken up by fools, a baleful influence from which escape is blessedly possible), and that intelligence should aspire to (and can attain) classlessness. He locates examples of classlessness in an American minority composed of "X-types"—certain "intellectuals ... actors, musicians, artists, sports stars, 'celebrities,' well-to-do former hippies, confirmed residers abroad, and the more gifted journalists" who extend an invitation to others to join them in breaking free from "the constraints and anxieties of the whole class racket."

The impatience and scorn concentrated in the phrase "the whole class racket" are organic to the assumption that class is something invented and perpetuated by swindlers. Fussell's style of taunting is in fact an American convention, turning up extensively in talk and print—no more often in books scolding extravagance than in advertising mediums selling $150 shirts and $100,000 ruby necklaces. Lewis Lapham mocks status-stupes willing to pay (and rustlers willing to charge) $23,000 a month for a two-bedroom suite at the Carlyle or $1,000 for a single, chicly catered dinner for four. George Will chides Rodeo Drive nits who, in the fantasied company of "stars," pay $42,000 for a fox fur bedspread. And the editors of *Avenue*, a magazine whose pages of shopping guides provide information about such items as evening bags for sale at $113,000, tease one of their pseudonymous columnists, Ms. Faux Pas, as a person seen racing for a fitting of "her $24,995 dress."

Impatience and scorn aren't the only feelings linked with

the assumption that class is a scam; there's also a certain wry satisfaction ("a fool and his money are soon parted"), and a lurking sense of class as a contagion—a disease known as "social pretension" spread by the silly and imprudent and easily contracted by the unwary. People ought to know better than to fool around with class, pushing themselves up, giving themselves airs. They're bound to be taken—deserve what they get—have to be thought of as suckers. It's a pity in a way. Almost a pity.

2. Class is temporary and various.

The American mobility credo asserts that children aren't limited by their parents' socioeconomic place, and that "background" is a springboard not a stocks; it clearly leads to doubt that social differences are hard, fast, and momentous. An undernoticed yet not minor tenet of the credo stresses social access, and it complicates the faith by adding variousness as a value. The impact is evident in political campaigns. By convention aspirants to high office claim humble origins, and by convention are needled for fibbing. (Wendell Willkie: "barefoot boy from Wall Street.") But the needling is gentle, sensitive to the sacral dimensions.

During the 1988 primary season Senator Gore disputed assertions that he belonged to the patriciate by noting he'd mucked out pig barns in his youth. In Iowa, separated from his own poor boy origins in Kansas by millions in trust funds and a Brooks Brothers fur-collared coat, Senator Dole asked voters to think to themselves: "Bob Dole is one of us." When reporters inquired about the fur-collared coat, the candidate exchanged it for plainer garb—and went on repeating the theme: I am one of you. He did so, probably, without feelings of deceit or cynicism. People strong in the mobility faith are no less ardent in their belief in multiple social identities; refusing to be pegged, they swiftly recover any previous level—even imaginary levels—of their social experience. The message communicated is that for those who in youth were strapped, in debt, without prospects, strapped-ness remains a permanent possibility of being. Manual labor performed in a distant yesterday remains alive forever in the bones. *(Been there, know what it's like to be you.)* Rising to celebrity and fortune from modest beginnings and thereafter treating one-time coevals as grotesques doesn't cancel fellow feeling; the repugnance momentarily in the celebrity's voice is to be registered as playacted, not real. What we were, we are; baggers *toujours.*

If the myth of the rise lacked this protean strain—if it consisted only of stories about legging it up the economic ladder—its capacity to energize the mind would be lower. But from age to age the promise of liberation from stuffy social inertia has charged the myth with glamour, adding the spice of nomadic fantasy to hopes of making it big. Nor does it matter that the myth overall lacks the grandeur of Whitman's dream (to be large, to contain multitudes). By conjoining success and variousness as icons, it manages to widen the social landscape and disencumber the mind. The patch of low metaphor in high places (a White House staffer speaks of "breaking his pick" on a tough assignment), the frequent looseness of gesture (a presidential candidate backpacking his garment bag), are among the numberless signs of its influence. So, too, is the broadly held suspicion that class identities are ambiguous and shifting, subject to overnight transformation, just possibly unreal.

This suspicion is one reason abusive class talk seems (to speakers and listeners alike) pardonable if not innocent. A maid is a maid—but she's also (perhaps) somebody about to be discovered. And she might be someone we once were (remember the motel job on the Cape just after freshman year? remember subbing for a roommate who worked the cleanup crew in the dining hall?) and therefore someone we could become again. Mortgaged and rooted in body we nevertheless retain picaresque souls: who knows where we'll be tomorrow?

3. *Class is a mask that genial good sense sees through.*
A culture valuing access and the absence of fixed levels can toy with the language of hierarchy and enjoy the frisson that accompanies any playfully subversive treatment of appearances as realities. But seriousness (not solemnity) returns, warning us not to trust surfaces, to dig a little deeper, and to avoid exaggerating social influences. For everyone who delights in *épater*ing the pious by talking hardnosed class, dozens exist who feel a modest civic obligation, when the subject of class comes up, to change the subject—move the discourse unobtrusively onto solider ground. This is done genially and casually, not fanatically, and out of respect for the truth that sensible people tend to prefer substance to shadow. Tone is everything on this front: no indicting of class as a racket or engaging in theorizing about the disposability of class. What happens is that class is simply brushed aside to permit clearer views. The process can occur consciously or unconsciously; it may or may not induce the sense of mild well-being that accompanies other affirmations of democratic virtues.

Many often-remarked peculiarities of American idiom can be traced to the penchant for treating class as camouflage—fog on the windowpane. The term *lifestyle*, introduced as useful shorthand for a variety of domestic living arrangements, achieved longevity because, as it incorporated consumer behavior into its range of reference, it obviated direct allusion to class. (Among American sociologists phrases such as "lifestyle enclaves" are now preferred alternatives to class-based terminology.) Many seldom-remarked peculiarities of American arts commentary are traceable to an insistence, by critics, on treating crucially important class dimensions of performers and talents as irrelevant trifles. Merce Cunningham and Michael Jackson give dance concerts the same night in Manhattan (Jackson is at Madison Square Garden). The younger performer's roots lie in pop, street dancing, the anguished history of an oppressed minority; the elder's roots lie in high art, classical ballet, the culture of the privileged. *The New York Times* assigns a critic who ordinarily works the snootier arts—Anna Kisselgoff—to review Michael Jackson, and her piece disposes of class in its lead. "Scrub away the veneer of street dances," writes Ms. Kisselgoff, "look past the occasional suggestive gesture and rotating pelvis, marvel at the backward gliding moonwalk and the isolated body parts ... and you see a virtuoso dancer who uses movement for its own sake. Yes, Michael Jackson is an avant garde dancer, and his dances could be called abstract. Like Merce Cunningham, he shows us that movement has a value of its own. . . ." Arguably, Jackson's social origins are a source of his strength and deserve better than to be thought of as dirt. But to admit this would be to admit that class matters—an un-American admission.

And the routine is the same when class impedes proper denigration, not appreciation. *People* magazine profiles a Southern collector of artifacts of twentieth-century American popular culture. The items in question originally belonged to working class blacks and whites in the region—individuals who paid money out of thin purses because the people and events that the objects commemorated were deeply meaningful to them. The objects were *infused* with the longings and ideals—also the sufferings and defeats—of those who bought them.

The Southern collector of the artifacts behaves and talks as though these associations were utterly without significance. He looks on an object that one can easily and unsentimentally imagine as expressive of genuine heartbreak—and genuine search for means of keeping hope alive in the face of heartbreak—and sees it in purely aesthetic terms; he praises it for its exceptionally pure vulgarity. *People* portrays him wincing as he holds up a "memorial religious clock" framed in grillwork and decorated with four oval insets of Jesus Christ and photographs of John and Robert Kennedy, Coretta and Martin Luther King. The article scrubs away the social context, concluding that the clock is a "lurid trinket." The collector comments: "Tacky just means tasteless." Class is dismissed.

In educational institutions the class-erasing impulse produces ever-changing coinages—"gifted," "over-achieving," "under-achieving," "slow," "special," and the like. And sooner or later admissions and counseling officers display restiveness with the clutter of social documentation that overwhelms them in applications ranging from those of offspring of professionals to those of children of royalty (Prince Rainier's heir, say) and of black cops in Queens. (The clutter includes data on parents' incomes, education, job titles; school records; autobiographical essays; statements of career interests; much more.) Once the new freshman class is chosen and folders bearing the accumulated documentation are passed along to faculty advisers, the bureaucracy signals its own boredom with the social mists by affixing a white label to the outside of each folder bearing one, pure, context-free item of information: the applicant's SAT scores.

According to educational researchers, family income is a considerably more helpful guide to students' academic needs and prospects than SAT scores. (If Grace Kelly's boy and a Queens cop's daughter score the same, their "learning aptitudes" are decidedly different.) But the neat labels strike through the mask, evoking hard science and neutral research. Scores are *scores*.

The assumption that class should be seen through whenever possible can produce embarrassments. A few years ago a sports TV personality and gambling-odds expert known as Jimmy the Greek involved himself in a complicated dispute arising partly from resentment, among African-Americans, about being excluded from top positions as coaches and managers, partly from allegations by whites that the ground of the exclusion was African-American intellectual deficiency. An issue of class difference seemed to be emerging in the dispute—but the gambling-odds expert gave an interview in which he claimed to see through the class dimensions to the genetic core. He argued that African-Americans, as slaves, had been *bred* with an eye to physical as opposed to mental distinction. The black athlete "has been bred to be better than whites because of his thigh size and his big size," quoth the Greek. "The slave owner would breed his big black to his big woman so that he would have a big black kid.... That's where it all started." The sports commentator meant not to cut his throat but to "explain" why blacks were unqualified for front office jobs and why whites were athletically mediocre, but the public protest greeting the publication of the interview finished him; he was fired from his network job.

The cause of the firing, though, was most definitely *not* the Greek's preference for genetic as opposed to class explanations of hierarchy. It was the flavor of racism that sank him (and his own low personal status). The down-to-earth tones and gestures customary in class unmasking—no-nonsense candor, distaste for red tape, concern for the bottom line—are seldom found objectionable. A maid is a maid, but she may have a shot at being discovered—and may have been interchangeable with ourselves—and her true identity may lie in genetics—or in "educational level"—or in SAT percentile.... The point being made is that her true identity lies anywhere on earth except in class.

Commutative laws apply to each of the foregoing assumptions. (Class is a ripoff because temporary, temporary because a ripoff, various because a mask, a mask because temporary, etc.) And, as is evident, the assumptions smoothly dissever class from power. Where preoccupation with class is found foolish and naive, where changing one's class is seen as feasible, where class is understood as really a disguise, class cannot be a major player in great undertakings. It's of the margins, peripheral; of the shadows, murky; a figment; a mirage.

At certain seasons, to be sure, during public discussion of "incomes" and "incomes policy," class peeps into sight as a force—a barrier or advantage. When tax laws are under revision, troublemakers will venture to shift discussion from brackets to wealth distribution, citing large percentages of national wealth held by small percentages of national population. Writers on the left periodically seek to reinvigorate the tradition of C. Wright Mills' *The Power Elite* (1956), a volume filled with reminders that American elites, like others, are homogeneous in class and education. And there are phrases in common use—"old boy network," "Eastern Establishment" and the like—that carry a hint of protest at the world of class connections.

But they carry stronger hints that the speakers wish to be seen as knowing (knowing about the personal relationships of power figures), or are convinced that old boys are inherently absurd. The classic American class stories invariably feature reversals in which an authority who thinks class matters is rudely shown that it doesn't. One favorite in the publishing industry is told about Cass Canfield, board chairman of Harper and Row in the Sixties. Enjoying postprandial cigars with a half dozen potent editors and publishers, young and old, Canfield listened quietly for a time to a conversation about jobs and class. One side held that publishing has too many Ivy Leaguers and establishmentarians. The other side said No. At length Canfield intervened, tut-tutting. But now really, said he, letting his glance pass over the six, we are, after all, the same, aren't we? All of us clubbable top dogs? All from the Ivy League? Whereupon came the class-unmasking turn that insures permanent popularity for the story. It emerged that only one of the six (a Yalie) was of the salt. The others without exception were bootstrap boys—characters who hailed from institutions and backgrounds totally lacking in cachet.

A heartening tale.

Class dismissed.

▪ *Chapter 3* ▪

THE IMPERIAL MIDDLE

The American population is composed not of classes but of men and women of the middle united as strivers and self-betterers.

Both the very rich and the very poor seek admission to the striving middle, and the poor are being accommodated as rapidly as facilities can be expanded.

*H*istorians and sociologists agree that during the nineteenth century a major change of opinion occurred concerning the composition of American society. Jefferson spoke for many when he wrote that people of "middling condition" were the country's saving force for equilibrium, balancing both the power-hungry rich and the helplessly ignorant poor. Implicit in this view was a model of a three-tiered republic stabilized by the practical wisdom of governors who, although indirectly educated by the responsible gentry, nevertheless came forth from the middle.

Within a half century, however, this model was considered to bear no resemblance to reality; the single division that had come to matter was, as Robert Wiebe puts it in *The Opening of American Society* (1985), between ins and outs. In the 1840s, "lacking gradations in a flattened society, respectable Americans ... drew a line—in or out—and concentrated on preserving their one significant distinction." Wiebe continues: "Above the class line lay the paths of progress that adults would choose if they could. Here, it was claimed, no one enjoyed privileges that others could not share, and everyone achieved a success equivalent to merit. Much of the tone of American society sustained that image of homogeneous enterprise."

No longer conceived of as a force restraining the immoderacies of both the rich and the propertyless, the middle gradually became—in popular thought and rhetoric—all-inclusive. In the late twentieth century, according to the sociologist Robert Bellah, the idea of process—of constant social motion—has completely replaced the idea of fixed class separations. But the movement toward that perspective was well under way a hundred years ago. By the late nineteenth century, the point of view of the emerging middle class was that "upper and lower classes fixed in some kind of equilibrium were illegitimate and, at best, temporary." Bellah himself believes that "the middle-class concept of an all-encompassing process of escalation that will eventually include everyone gives us our central, and largely unchallenged, image of American society."

The actual processes of change—the genesis and development of the attitudes of the "ins"—are an important element, obviously, in the creation of the psyche of classlessness; a subsequent chapter will look carefully at them. But the present focus isn't upon origins and causes, or upon differences between then and now, but rather on what *is*—con-

THE IMPERIAL MIDDLE • 43

temporary feelings and attitudes. The most significant among the latter, perhaps, are those shaped by assumptions about the composition of American society.

1. *The American population is composed not of classes but of men and women of the middle united as strivers and self-betterers.*

The mind of the middle isn't absorbed with the subject of class, doesn't engage ceaselessly in placing itself and others, and lives without detailed maps of social difference. But those in concord with this mind aren't without conceptions of themselves and others in social terms, and often have strong, clear feelings about the differences that finally insist upon recognition.

The people in question know, for instance, that although they may sometimes speak of themselves as men or women of the "middle class," only with an effort of will—only by contrivance—can they imagine themselves to *be* members of a class. Normally they feel themselves to be solid individual achievers in an essentially classless society composed of human beings engaged in bettering themselves. The society thus pictured isn't regarded as without faults; most assuredly it needs more heart; but pleasure can be taken in it because, on balance, it is ... very nearly classless.

Opinion on this point has different foundations at different stages of human lives. At one moment it may be rooted in a personal experience of upward mobility; at another it derives from feelings of having won out—succeeded in maintaining a middle level of existence over a lifetime. (How easy it is to be dislodged from a perch when class is constantly shifting! What else can it have been but my *effort*—not any fixity in the class system itself—that's made the difference!)

But realization of the essential classlessness of society

doesn't foster denials of all difference. To the contrary: men and women of the striving middle know that, while not members of a class, they are sharply separated from at least some of the others. Real differences exist. They have to do with intelligence (taste, culture) and character (moral fiber, mental discipline). If the Others were smarter, everyone would be interchangeable. If they were stronger-willed and better at delaying gratification, all would be one. If they but knew how to discriminate between excellence and mediocrity, style and vulgarity, culture and junk, tasteful and tacky, difference would disappear.

And in time difference will disappear, because people of the striving middle care. They are compassionate—anything but blind to social problems. They have sympathy for the poor, aliens, homeless, abused children, hardluck farmers, "people left behind in the yuppie years"—even for the criminals, addicts, diseased and their young who have lately come to be spoken of (the term communicates the shared sense of their mysteriousness) as "the underclass." The middle is especially moved by news show segments about formerly well-situated people who have somehow lost their doorman apartments and landed in the street. Action is indicated. Conceivably there are hundreds of thousands—perhaps millions—of such cases, or accidents: strange tales, stories of personal misfortune. Often the stories have to do with individuals who, sadly, weren't provident (or quite bright enough); sometimes they are downright tragic. But the stories aren't essentially about different classes or class cultures, because difference on that scale—of that *kind*—doesn't really exist. Norms, values, responses to problems are pretty much the same all over.

Challenges occur, to be sure—some eruption or other

of psychopathic behavior, such as a mass murder, that momentarily shakes trust in the essential comprehensibility and uniformity of the social landscape. But the same newspapers that shake the trust on Monday restore it by the weekend. EXPERTS SAY MASS MURDERS ARE RARE BUT ON RISE, reads the headline in *The New York Times* a few days after a pair of shattering tragedies. The respectfully quoted experts include a University of Virginia psychiatrist who consults for the FBI, and two criminologists at Boston and Northeastern universities. Each takes positions denying the need to imagine authentically different responses to life—attitudes, levels of rage, grounds for embitterment remote from the common run. "I never came across [a mass murderer]," says the psychiatrist, "who wasn't at least partially interested in suicide. They have a very limited view of options, such as a career change, divorce, or declaring bankruptcy." They don't know, says the expert, that "depression is very common and easily treated."

The language states explicitly that problems outside the familiar middle mode don't exist. The would-be murderer should do as strivers and self-betterers do—call and make an appointment with his analyst and with his tax accountant (think Chapter 11) and with his marriage counselor. Bonded to each other, the newspaper, the experts, the audience assimilate the mass murderer to the norm.

And this is merely one among a myriad of styles of assimilation. Some styles are direct: columns by George Will assert that "the working class" is, "to most Americans, as foreign as Mongolia," and that nobody "not crazy" dares to ride New York subways. Some styles assimilate by intimation, as when lead articles in "Home" sections of newspapers discuss, for an urban audience of a million, the desirability of inheriting fine furniture as opposed to shopping for it.

Few publications more revealingly mirror the striving middle's confidence in the homogeneity of things than re-union classbooks, wherein college friends ruminate on their personal projects, states of mind, attitudes toward "prob-lems," opinions about the social order and how it should change. "Nobody," protests a concerned member of a recent Radcliffe twenty-year class, "nobody sees it as their business if someone doesn't have enough to eat or doesn't quite fit into normal society." The language neatly miniaturizes the unassimilated and personalizes the "issues." A few miscella-neous misfits need feeding and the problem is that "normal society" is too huge and self-involved to notice.

"My latest extracurricular project," writes a lawyer who reports that his nearest neighbor lives a mile away, is "to persuade Vermont to add an amendment to its constitution which declares 'That the people have a right to privacy which is essential to their freedom and shall be preserved.' " If the social order consists of "normal society" and a few misfits, who could deny that the dearth of privacy deserves priority on agendas for social change? In the classbooks the voice of the striving middle regularly defines "maturity" as an under-standing that "the problems of society" are in fact problems of individual moral nature and are unrelated to conflicts of interest or class. "I am less ready to see individual or 'class' villains," writes Christopher St. John, Harvard '67, "and a little more sadly accepting of the weak, ignorant, and self-deceiving aspects of our natures."

All give offense equally, including ourselves; all therefore are one.

2. Both the very rich and the very poor seek admission to the striving middle, and the poor are being accommo-dated as rapidly as facilities can be expanded.

On its face this assumption seems wobbly. Granted, an imperial middle exists: surely the *very* rich and the *very* poor lie beyond its engrossment? Can even an imperial middle believe itself to be *all*?

One reason the very rich seem assimilable, if not digestible, is that the representatives of new fortunes who become visible keep inspiring, in the striving middle, an absolutely unfaked sense of the inferiority of the rich. No trace of latent envy or sour grapes enters the response of aversion triggered by a Donald Trump or Leona Helmsley; the feelings are impersonal yet deep, and not untinged with pity. It is, after all, a fearful punishment for a human creature to be at once this unattractive and this vain, this conceited and this inept, this preceptorial and this witless. If the very rich are different, then the difference is (given the evidence) so incontrovertibly for the worse, not the better, that hierarchy is convulsed.

And the convulsion is worsened by the increasing willingness of old fortunes to allow themselves to be seen behaving in ways that are death to awe—witness a David Rockefeller party for the late Sekou Touré, dictator of Guinea and slaughterer of 100,000 of his countrymen, described by Lewis Lapham, a guest:

"At the luncheon with the Rockefellers, Touré's wife was dressed in a white mink hat and a white mink coat which dragged becomingly along the floor. Rockefeller welcomed Touré with an elaborate toast, saying that when he was last in Conakry, Touré had met him at the airport in a Mercedes limousine and that on their subsequent drive through the streets of the city Touré dispensed with the services of a chauffeur. Miracle of miracles, Touré had driven the car himself. To Rockefeller this proved that Touré was a great African leader, a man of the people who had taken to heart the immortal lessons of democracy.... After luncheon Rockefeller ordered one of his nineteenth-century carriages brought around to the front door, and he set jauntily off, driving the horses himself, with Mrs. Touré beside him on the box and Touré seated in back with Mrs. Rockefeller."

If there were signs that the obscurer rich were quietly maintaining standards and values worthy of respect yet remote from those of the general culture, the imperial middle might question its own sway. But repeatedly the obscurer rich are caught out in situations dramatizing the fragility of their sense of self. They seem actually to cower before the middle, tormenting themselves with middle-style dreams of achievement and betterment, in some instances bribing the middle in hope of being awarded respectable social identities. A pair of Texas millionaires recently paid the Kennedy School of Government $500,000 for titles at Harvard that are "normally reserved for instructors and administrators." The agreement stipulated that in return for the money, Charles C. Dickinson III and Joanne W. Eaton Dickinson of Wichita Falls, Texas, would be "appointed to appropriate positions in the School of Government that will afford them status as Officers of the University with the privileges associated therewith. . . ." The AP quoted Mrs. Dickinson as saying: "Charles and I need an identity. We cannot very well say we are philanthropists at cocktail parties. We want to be affiliated with Harvard."

Pathetic, indeed—but not astonishing. In the face of the imperial middle's immense confidence in the non-existence of values and standards different from its own, heroism alone can bear to be merely philanthropic.

It is a truism that, because the imperial middle's assurance of the uniformity of the whole abides no question, problems of shaky social identity can arise; it is a cruel paradox that the problems are not limited to the very rich. As the reports of caseworkers time and again confirm, the very poor quite commonly arraign themselves as undeserving—as people momentarily lost, perhaps about to be found. Pressed to perceive the imperial middle's norms as all-inclusive, they concur in the proposition that their own marginality and non-participation result from personal faults, moral or intellectual. Not long ago *The New York Times* carried a feature story about a fifteen-year-old named Mark Jenkins who lives in Chicago's notorious Cabrini Green housing project and attends Lincoln Park, one of the city's top public schools. The story reported that Jenkins is the only member of his family who works (he gets up at 6 A.M. to hawk newspapers on street corners), and that, on his way to school, he dodges crossfire between rival gangs fighting outside his apartment building. Jenkins met his father for the first time when he was twelve ("my grandmother showed me to him and we shook hands"). The boy hopes to get to college and hungers to make it out of Cabrini Green ("I don't want to go around broke"); at the time the story was filed, prospects were bad: he was failing several classes and a paperboy layoff was about to cost him his job.

The detail in this familiar story that lent it singularity concerned the boy's personal explanation of his difficulties. After observing Jenkins at school and querying him about his attitudes, the reporter wrote: "In the [school] hallways, Mark passes middle-class white and black students wearing Harvard T-shirts and imagines that they live in nice homes and don't have to dodge bullets to get to school. He says they deserve to live better than he does because 'they're smarter than me.' "

Movies provide glimpses now and then of white working class men and women awakening suddenly to awareness of the intensity of the desire around them for oneness with the middle. Such a scene occurred in *Blue Collar* (1978); the awakening came to Harvey Keitel, cast as an auto worker. In one sequence the camera fastens tight on his face as he stares uncomprehendingly at his daughter, having discovered that she's mutilated her mouth with homemade wire braces. The child dreamed of membership in her school marching corps, and was rejected as a drum majorette because of buck teeth. (There was no money in the family budget for orthodontics.) Feelings come to Keitel, the father, in a rush—helplessness, pity, confusion, anger, awe.

And one's ability to feel with him may well depend on personal experience, as in my case. No child of mine has mutilated herself, to be sure, but one taught me compellingly about the force of human longings for a place in the middle. The time was the Fifties. We had just moved to a moderately genteel faculty house warren in the small New England college town where I taught, and were hard up—burdened with graduate school debt. Happy with new friends, our daughter imitated their ways, innocently seeking to put a bit of distance between herself and her strapped and faintly "peculiar" parents. I was prickly with the families of the new friends, thin-skinned about my own cultural as well as financial indigence, and not yet a committed academician. They seemed not only effete and pretentious—like the graduate students at Harvard some had once been—but starchy and churchy as well. Very churchy.

So we quarreled: sensitive, clever, plucky ten-year-old versus raw, self-protective, early-thirtyish father. The content was predictable. Why couldn't we just once go to church as a family—just once, just Easter? What difference did it make that the church of *my* youth was Methodist, not Episcopal, if there wasn't any Methodist church here? When we took her to Sunday School, why did we have to drop her off on the side street instead of where others stopped? Why couldn't she have white sandals now? You needed them, you had to *have* them. Everybody ...

Banal stuff. But a moment arrived—an event I heard of but did not witness—that still stings in memory. A friend told us what had happened on the Sunday morning when our daughter volunteered to *sing* in the Grace Episcopal church choir. Dropped off as usual at the church's side entrance, white-sandaled and begloved, she made her way alone through the choir-loft passage and, presenting herself to the choir director, announced that she would like to join the choir. She *loved* to sing, she could read music.... The choir director, a Mrs. Morgan, was rich, artsy, and Anglophile, a member of the Puritan Waspdom with which I was somewhat smolderingly ill-at-ease.

"Well, dear child," said she to my daughter. "That's very nice. We'd love having you. But you see—really we don't have a robe for you."

Jo's eyes filled, according to our friend. All at once our proud non-weeper was weeping.

Mrs. Morgan stared in unbelief.

"Oh dear, of *course*," said she. "But now don't fret. I'm sure we'll find an old robe somewhere. Come next week."

She patted my daughter's shoulder once, and turned away. Cool New England comfort and dismissal.

I see the gesture still and remember still my feelings (confusion, anger, helplessness) on hearing of it. How could my child need *them* so badly as to beg their pity? Why had I let self-involvement blind me to her need?

* * *

American assumptions about society in the large commingle comfortably with American assumptions about class (those that were treated in the last chapter); together they function capitally as social emollients and sedatives. By their action a nation comes to exist, in tens of millions of imaginations, as a family. Yale students and greasers rise as one in standing ovations for Springsteen; daytime bigots become, in prime time, tolerant and kind, enjoying *The Cosby Show* and moderating their "prejudice"; within the borders peace reigns.

As does the troubling condition of unwitting confinement. Means of overcoming the confinement aren't readily available. A faculty child's tears—fear of rejection, fear that the curse of her parents' eccentricity and poverty will bear upon her forever—are neither indecipherable nor, in the large scheme of things, weighty. Elsewhere, though, gravity and urgency can attend emotions and behavior rooted in class differences, and the pursuit of understanding is difficult. The behavior of high school boys at their physical exam for the wartime draft, a quarter-century ago, differed with large consequences from that of college boys: where to begin the hunt for clues to the difference? The feelings of the black lad at poolside who dove and, not knowing how to swim, drowned, differed from those of the freshmen who stood larking beside him: how are those differences best probed? The responses of crew to foreman differ from those of foreman to crew, and from those of foreman to supervisor, and from those of supervisor to production chief.

And no less unique are the responses of the "bad" child to the teacher and guidance counselor who inform him suddenly that—"for your own good, not as a punishment"—he will now depart for a "special class," in another school, separated forever from his fifth-grade friends. In these and hundreds of other instances, no satisfactory understanding of what is taking place, and why, can be reached except under the aegis of a constructive imagination that's both well informed about and passionately engaged with the realities of class difference. Yet more often than not, even by those officially deputed to elucidate such events, the subject of class goes unmentioned.

In the absence of a firmly defined human situation, tragic or otherwise, knowing where to start—how to begin framing questions that help to bring difference alive—isn't easy, as I said. In my view two steps are essential. The first is to grasp that the substance of class in contemporary America concerns differences in people's actual physical, mental, imaginative activity as workers, differences in what people come to learn and master in the course of their general lives, differences in levels of self-respect, and differences in the visions of life possibility that attain vivid meaning for people as family members and as participants in larger communities. The second essential step is to realize that, although these differences are less immediately visible than those of income or consumer spending, and although they resist formulation under the crude rubrics of class warfare, they are nevertheless profoundly significant and warrant scrupulous regard by all who teach, govern, judge, or otherwise claim deference from their fellows.

But for a while this matter of the precise nature of existing class differences in our midst can be laid aside. Just now the pressing question concerns *how*—in our times, when heedlessness of rents in the social fabric seems nearly impossible; in our cities, where blindness to difference seems inconceivable—how the theme of the imperial middle as All manages to survive. According to old sayings, myth and dream live off the land they occupy—but that land seems in some sense worked out, can no longer feed from its bounty the dream of classless America. How, then, is the dream nourished? Who provides?

· Part II ·

THE MEDIA: ARTS OF EXORCISM AND ERASURE

·

▪ *Chapter 4* ▪

APPEARANCE, REALITY, RENUNCIATION

*O*ne part of the explanation of how the idea of classlessness is nourished is that significant branches of industry—information, advertising, and entertainment, and not uncommonly the higher arts as well—provide sustenance. They labor jointly to soften the edges of social difference. Both instinct and design guide the labor, many aspects of which are well known. Everyone is aware, for instance, that TV commercials (except those for sneakers) portray upscale middle class consumers enjoying recognizably middle class pleasures ("Would you like to go out for a banana split?"), and that TV news organizations recruit on-camera teams for local and national broadcasts from among candidates who look prosperous—not pinched. (The longest-surviving socially "wrong" face at one network—that of Ike Pappas, Pentagon correspondent—was reportedly perceived as having a "blue-collar look"; Pappas was severed in the mid-Eighties.)

It's also well known that, in representing the country's social makeup, the news industry habitually enlarges the imperial middle. As Columbia sociology professor Herbert Gans notes, the press banishes the lower middle class—"the skilled and semi-skilled white-collar workers who are, next to blue-collar workers, the largest class in America, however they are labeled." Furthermore, Gans adds, by "eschewing the term 'working class,' the news also brings blue-collar workers into the middle class; and by designating upper middle-class people as middle class, it makes them appear to be more numerous than they actually are."

These class mergers are buttressed, in turn, by editorial commentary. Columnists find frequent occasion to remark on the universality of affluence and the disappearance of the working class. Humorists treat the rich as marginal eccentrics whose queer habits deserve pity. (Lewis Grizzard is sorry for poloists and old stodgies who dine out in jackets and ties.) Even pollsters contribute to the homogenization, by sorting out differences of opinion in ways that shrink income categories at the lower and upper ends of the spectrum. During the last presidential campaign *The New York Times*–CBS tabulations placed interviewees in five income categories: "Under $12,500; $12,500–25,000; $25,000–35,000; $35,000–50,000; over $50,000"; only one of these categories—"under $12,500—lay unambiguously outside the borders of the middle as usually conceived.

The result of these and other practices and devices is a difference-dissolving background into which evidence of variegation recedes. But the media provide more than mere background for the sustenance of "classless" society. They provide basic bread-and-butter stories about individuals and families establishing—in contemporary terms—the non-existence of class. Working with and through the dominant commercial, political, and performing celebrities, they update democratic man and woman, creating new images of ideal American sociopsychological being that quiet fears that the society is stratified. With the aid of the professions, the media hone languages that mask or transform class realities by representing them in non-class terms. And by regularly transforming class differences into moral and intellectual differences, the media provide the imperial middle with a massive stimulus to vanity.

Yesterday's rags-to-riches success stories held a mirror up to social existence, offering people versions of what was happening around them that affirmed the American Dream and possessed unifying power. Almost from its beginnings movie comedy possessed the same power, partly because of what one critic—James Harvey—has called its reliably consistent "animus against gentility." Comparably optimistic social messages continue to be sent today in numberless thousands of hours of entertainment programming (sitcoms, cop shows, teenie flicks, other forms). The reassuring word passed in these stories is that American society remains faithful to its first promise, classless and homogeneous at its core.

They're not, however, rags-to-riches stories, nor are they deeply hostile to the genteel. The idea of ascent has been modified and three newish story patterns have emerged. The first pattern stresses discovery; characters who think firm class lines exist discover they're mistaken. A second pattern involves upendings: characters theoretically on the social bottom prove their superiority to characters theoretically on the social top. The third pattern dramatizes renunciations: characters belonging to the middle who are momentarily tempted by lofty visions of social/cultural ascent reject the temptation, realizing there are no higher satisfactions than those they already possess.

The stories in which one or more of these often overlapping patterns appear can be bare or elaborate, structurally—shells on which to pin laugh lines, or intricately organized narratives in which full-fledged subplots comment on social messages in the main action. Always the difference-dissolving background of network news and ads reenforces the basic themes of the stories. But the stories themselves matter most.

Consider *The Cosby Show*. In tonight's segment the joke is on Cliff and Clare Huxtable, upscale black professionals (doctor and lawyer). At the start of the program Cliff and Clare behave as though they're living not in wide-open America but in a class society; during the half hour, helped by their kids, they grasp their mistake.

Things happen as follows:

In the opening frames the parents are seen rejoicing in a piece of good social fortune. Their oldest child, Sondra, a Princeton senior, has just married Alvin, a Princeton classmate; Sondra has been admitted to law school, Alvin to med school. Cliff and Clare, parents and in-laws of winners, beam at each other: "They'll be following in our footsteps," "going to good graduate schools," starting where they deserve. They display the sendoff presents they've bought for "our future professionals"—a fine stethoscope engraved with the message "Straight From My Heart," a gold-embossed briefcase.

Comes a bombshell. The Princeton newlyweds arrive and reveal they're not going to graduate school. Alvin has discovered that, "philosophically," he has "a problem with charging sick people money" for taking care of them, and anyway doesn't want to "spend the next eight years in school"; he's taken a job in a pill-bottling plant. Sondra has also "changed my mind"; she has a job as a waitress.

Rage entertainingly ensues. Cliff snarls ("I think it stinks"), Clare explodes: "After all the money we spent sending you to Princeton!" she cries. "You owe us $79,000! Empty her pockets!" One scene later, on a visit to the youngsters' low-rent apartment—tumbledown furniture, neon signs blaring in the window—the parents learn that Alvin's bottling-factory job has fallen through and he's awaiting an opening as busboy where Sondra waits tables. Cliff slow-burns hilariously, teeth clenched: "I let him marry my daughter because he was going to be a *doctor.*"

No lasting problem, naturally: we're in sitcom country. It emerges that the Princetonians haven't opted to become layabouts; they have a "five-year plan" for amassing venture capital by living frugally and saving. The capital will be used to open a "wilderness store" in which, after training in a similar place operated by their friends, they'll work side by side. The parents simmer down as they listen. Clare, who a minute before had been telling Cliff to take the son-in-law into the real wilderness and "drop him off," now says: "They're moving ahead very well." Cliff for his part seems impressed to learn, in one-on-one conversation with Alvin, that the youngster's head is stored with business success stories, several of which concern the ups and downs of the founder of Hershey chocolate. Chastened, he offers the couple aid ("I'd like to help out.... Take it as a loan").

The show's kicker gives us the Huxtables' only son, a high schooler named Theo who's been observing events, attempting to do a deal. Theo proposes to his parents that they pay him $112,500 today, his estimate of the probable cost of his undergraduate education; in exchange he'll skip college, sparing them worries about whether he'll become yet another grad school dropout. The lad's mother suggests he leave the room while still alive.

Now this.

Often praised for providing improving images of American life, *The Cosby Show* abolishes differences between majority and minority cultures. Black and white families are essentially the same in its depiction. Both spend heavily for consumer goods (clothes, furniture, stereos, VCRs), both share the same aims for their children (professional careers in medicine and law), both have excellent prospects of realizing these ambitions (no members of the Huxtable family, young or old, ever meet with obstacles in the form of discrimination that impede their efforts as striving individualists). Without preaching, lecturing, or straying from the subject of parents and kids, seldom missing a chance to smile at the gap between youngsters' impulsive looniness and grownups' inefficacious rationality, the show creates the wide-open society.

Thursdays at 8 P.M., before an audience of forty-five million, Princeton boys become busboys. Blacks with a chance to start at the summit elect to start at the bottom. Waitresses aren't waitresses, they're accumulating venture capital. Achievers who battle their way into the Ivy League, fight for A's, make it into professional schools, chuck everything and light out for the frontier, or frontier store. Thursdays at 8 the population is composed of two kinds of people, individualistic strivers (Cliff, Clare, Sondra, and Alvin are, regardless of career choices, strivers) and goofoffs (for the moment Theo is a goofoff, but who knows? He could become a professor one day, or perhaps a brilliant comic, such as Bill Cosby). And the sole governing principle is that of unpredictability.

People do forget these truths, the show admits; they fall into the error of fretting about lines, bars, fixities of rank. Cliff and Clare themselves behave for a while as though the country were a place wherein well-off parents pass along advantages to children eager to have them because aware that (1) the top is the place to be, (2) top spots are largely inherited, (3) the American Dream (everybody equal, everybody striving) is bunk. Cliff talks as though clear gaps separate not only physicians from plant hands but plant hands from busboys; Clare talks as though clear gaps separate UN guides—the job she hoped Sondra would get, once law school was rejected —from waitresses.

But—meat of the tale—they wake up. By the end it's plain that, hereabouts, life is fluid, hospitable to overnight change. Concern about status is senseless because status is ever in flux: this is the U.S. of A., no permanent edges or impairments allowed.

Light entertainment, unpretentious, often saccharine, occasionally charming, *The Cosby Show* isn't about stratification theory; it's about gorgeous family members in animated, mugging and teasing interaction. Each week a fresh version of the spirited infighting of parents and kids, and never a sermon on American Social Reality. But the laugh lines are strung on a message, simple, immediate, pleasing. Princeton is no Big Deal, nor is a silver spoon or advanced degree. For every single one of us it's a roller coaster out there: ask Bill Cosby.

Stories for general or family audiences, like *The Cosby Show*, tend to concentrate on the reactions of those observing the roller coaster from at least temporarily solid ground. Stories for smaller, sharply defined audiences evoke mid-ride experiences of people on board. And a key element in the experiences is pleasure in seeing overconfident top dogs get their comeuppance and bottom dogs moving briefly but exhilaratingly to the top.

As in the films of John Hughes—love stories in which golden-skinned, foulmouthed yet virginal teen kings and queens frolic in lush suburban schoolyards reverberant with rock soundtracks. Heavy grossers in the malls, Hughes' movies center on poor boy/poor girl fantasies of ascendancy by omnicompetence. Their working class heroes or heroines become romantically interested in classmates who rank above them, in terms of money and status, in school society. And as the attachments develop, the poorer kids commence to display gifts and talents that prove them equal or (more often) intrinsically superior to the arrogant, insecure characters in whom they've become interested. After the true, nonclass order or hierarchy has been established, and superficial, class-based gradations have been reversed, the poor boy or girl chooses whether to continue the relationship with the pseudo-superior or to end it and return to the original social situation. Either way the total experience bolsters belief that, in school and out, strata are evanescent and meaningless. The roller coaster is waiting, for the poor as for the rich; the sole requirement for admission is the impulse to climb on.

Keith, the eighteen-year-old poor-boy hero of Hughes' *Some Kind of Wonderful* (1987), pumps gas after school, has no college plans, and is accustomed to being treated scornfully by the rich classmates who swoop into the station in Corvettes and blast their horns in his ear ("Sorry, it was an accident," said with a smirk), while he's checking their oil. ("Be nice to me," says a richie meanly, "or I'll make you check the tires.") But one day Keith finds himself drawn to Amanda Jones, "who runs with the rich and beautiful." And

APPEARANCE, REALITY, RENUNCIATION • *65*

as his curiosity about Amanda strengthens, his hitherto inconspicuous qualities and talents emerge—qualities that set him a notch higher than the richies who condescend to him and behave possessively toward Amanda.

The talents are various. A mechanic good enough to restore classic cars, Keith is also an artist specializing in abstract canvases, and a teenage sophisticate who, despite humble family origins, is worldly and poised in posh settings (on a date with Amanda he selects a *luxo* restaurant, orders wine and Beluga caviar). His unfailing good manners to rude rich kids reflect personal style, not craven subservience. The boy who says *please* and *thank you* to moneyed louts who blast their horns intentionally while he's under the hood is also a Clever Trickster who understands it's better to get even than to get mad. As one hornblaster pulls away, we see Keith neatly deposit the dipstick of the character's Corvette in a rubbish can.

What's more, Keith is an effortlessly masterful politico. When a group of richies plots to punish him physically for dating one of "their" girls, he gathers a gang of greaser-bruisers to his side—they respect him as an outsider, hence one of them—to fend off the would-be assailants. This bottom dog owes no man or woman deference, in short; cinchy for him to oppress his oppressors. Riding the roller coaster from start to finish as unconditioned man, he ceaselessly exercises free choice. After Amanda, who hitherto ran with the rich, decides she'd be pleased to run with him, Keith decides he's happier with Watts, his longtime tomboy girlfriend, and, by mutual consent, he and Amanda break up. But neither this nor any other act of his constitutes knuckling under to the social system.

Pop custom dictates that characters like Keith who know

better than to believe in class will be surrounded by characters sunk in superstition on the subject. Voices keep warning Keith that a social system exists that can hurt him. (The voices resemble, in some respects, those of the elder Huxtables expressing outrage at their kids' temporary embrace of downward mobility.) Father, sister, and tomboy girlfriend struggle to keep Keith in the fold, away from what the girlfriend calls the "big money, cruel heart society" alleged to be capable of destroying him. The richies, in turn, ostracize Amanda Jones for dating him. But Keith's example teaches Amanda not to be intimidated, and in separate ways each wins at the end.

And the story is the same in other Hughes' films. *Pretty in Pink* (1986) features an omnicompetent poor-girl heroine who, at the close, accepts a pleading richie. *The Breakfast Club* (1985) draws together a quintet of superficially class-divided high schoolers for a day of detention; before their release the five students create a classless utopia for themselves. The message is unvarying: the surface of things may look structured, and some members of the society may talk themselves into believing that escape from fixed levels is impossible, but actually where we place ourselves is up to us; whenever we wish to, we can upend the folks on the hill. Eat your heart out, George Steinbrenner. Down from that tower, Donald Trump.

Renunciation stories, as might be guessed, tend to be more complicated than tales of upending or awakening. During several recent seasons the most touching renunciation stories on TV centered on the character of Marybeth Lacey in *Cagney and Lacey*, a cop series whose six-year run ended in 1988. Friends and fellow police officers, the two heroines

of the show were imagined as people of different class background. Lacey, brunette, Queens-accented, married to Harv
and the mother of two sons, was self-respecting working class;
as a child she helped her harried mom fight the battle for
respectability, cooking, cleaning, coping. Cagney, blond, single, college-educated, had a privileged past (her father, a police officer, married up). Lacey once remarked that when her
mother was taking her to the Music Hall, Cagney's mother
was taking Cagney to the Russian Tea Room and the sym-
phony.

On and off the job the two women often quarreled—
and character differences figured in the disputes. Cagney was
the impatient, incautious risktaker, demonstrative and prone
to hasty judgment; Lacey was calmer, more contained and
undemanding—a solid, practical sort, although quicker than
Cagney to tears. Shot-selection highlighted, in Cagney, an
uninhibited, armswinging broadness of gesture and a chal-
lenging set of the mouth; Lacey's physicality was less animated
and her speech less impetuous. But dialogue regularly led
back to social roots; downwardly mobile Cagney's recklessness bespoke the confidence and self-absorption that accompanies privilege, Lacey's inhibitions (except in bed) and
wariness reflected the survivalist instincts of the less well off.
Socially charged clashes of taste were frequent. (When Cagney cast incidental contempt on *Little House on the Prairie*,
Lacey defended the show: "That program is good entertainment, Christine.")

And Lacey was often entranced by aspects of Cagney's
difference—her boldness, emotional freedom, careless
cultivation—and tempted to probe for herself the promise
of the larger life implicit in that difference. Strong as the
temptation became, however—powerfully as Lacey some-

times longed to venture out from the nest of her securities —good sense invariably took command, showing her that the so-called finer things to which her partner had access weren't as fine as the life she herself already lived. And the differences in the partners' backgrounds never seriously disturbed their friendship. Reconciliations and renewals of affection followed every spat; the cycle underlined the relative insignificance of the class differences dramatized in the course of the hour.

An episode: a well-known abstract painter donates a picture to a children's hospital benefit. The work is stolen and Cagney and Lacey are assigned to the case. After talking with the artist in his studio, they begin questioning some gallery owners. For Cagney galleries are old turf ("I used to do this all the time"); she remembers gallery-hopping when this particular artist—named Greenlow—was an unknown ("My junior year in France I could have had a Greenlow for nothing"). Speaking French with gallery owners gives her moderate pleasure, as does summoning the appropriate clichés of remembered introductory fine arts courses ("silent poetry" and the like), and displaying acquaintance with technical vocabularies remote from police work. But it's evident that her aestheticism is school-sponsored, school-learned; forced back into touch with it she experiences *déjà vu*, not excitement.

For Marybeth Lacey, though, the gallery world hums with revelations. Pictures and people alike intrigue her; we feel her nascent awe and sense of exclusion as her partner becomes, thanks to her French, jauntily refined—and produces correct names for materials and processes. The scenes faintly echo nineteenth-century themes—the glamour of art and learning ... the capacity of art to intimate, to certain imaginations, the existence of a better world, grander human hopes ... the difference between art as a "course" or tour and art as an inner dawning of the *promesse du bonheur*. Lacey's sudden hesitations with her partner—eager deference, shameless pressing of questions, helpless desire—are affecting. Cagney's defensive, half-proud, half-embarrassed responses, on the other hand, are troubling. Shaking off the would-be learner's importunacy ("Can we have a recess?"), she flatly mocks the questions ("Christine, what is impasto?" "An Italian sauce made with pesto").

But mockery can't reach Lacey. Unlike characters in up-ending stories, this heroine hungers for nothing attainable by snapping omnicompetent fingers. The French words tripping gently from her partner's lips, and her new awareness of art as a kind of knowledge inspire in the policewoman-mother an ambition to study—a will to drive herself to qualify for entry into the temple of cultivation. And in time the ambition comes across fully to others. Even Lacey's loving but exhausted husband, disposed initially to worry about the inconvenience of having a mate entering college in mid-life, is moved to promise cooperation, once he feels the force of Lacey's awakened aspiration.

Yet the program *is* a renunciation story; before the end Lacey sees through her desire to become like her privileged partner and rejects seduction by polylingual cultivation. The spurning is prepared for in subplots which, as an hour-long show, *Cagney and Lacey* comfortably accommodated. One subplot, focused on Christine Cagney and a new male friend, a plumber, stresses that relationships are damaged when one partner takes "culture" more seriously than the other. (Nick, the plumber, walks out on Cagney the minute he suspects her of trying to broaden his cultural horizons: "You can't make me into a Brooks Brothers man." *Will Harv walk out on Lacey?*) Another subplot, centered on Lacey and the artist

Greenlow, stresses that artists are immorally self-centered—producers of toys for the privileged, not sources of true inspiration for ordinary people. (Artist: "I paint for the rich." Lacey: "That's not enough.") When, toward the close of the show, Lacey repudiates her aspirations, she doesn't cite her experience with the artist as a reason. But the early intimation that the world of art isn't the utopia she first imagined—may actually be coldly unmoved by human suffering—helps to ready the audience for the reversal.

Its terms, not surprisingly, are simple. Lacey gradually cottons to the truth that the finer things are invitations to inauthenticity and that her own appetite for them springs from vanity and selfishness. Husband Harv patiently re-educates her in the blessings at hand, and in the comparative emptiness of the life—Christine Cagney's life—that she's mistakenly envied. Cagney speaks idiomatic French, but has no children. (She "couldn't be a mother," Lacey reflects, sad for her friend.) Husband and wife turn the pages of a photo album, pausing over a shot of their kids. "Are you telling me this isn't as precious as a Picasso?" asks Harv. The melting expression on Lacey's face announces the end of Marybeth the Obscure's fantasy of rising. The life we of the middle possess is richer by far than any available to the artsy-fartsy; cultural ambitions only imperil it.

Story patterns are abstractions; the personalities of players are tangible. Hawkeye (Alan Alda) in *M*A*S*H*, Dolly Parton in *Nine to Five*, the Eddie Murphy character in Murphy movies, the uppity young black lawyer who, in *L.A. Law*, outwits the Establishment on his first day in court, the hero of *Back to the Future*—these bear no immediately discernible resemblance either to each other or to Keith in John Hughes'

Some Kind of Wonderful. Finding the common strand—seeing these and scores of related characters as Clever Tricksters adept at upending figures who lord it over them—requires a step back from persons to paradigm. Similar acts of detachment are required to uncover the links between, say, Pizza Man Frank Furillo's downwardly mobile girlfriend in *Hill Street Blues* and downwardly mobile Frasier of Harvard in *Cheers* —or the connections between the waitress-student Diane's renunciation of cultural ambition in *Cheers* (in the Shelley Long era) and similar renunciations in *thirtysomething* or *Cagney and Lacey.*

And the detached stance isn't one with which decency is always at ease. (The right response to programs that persuasively cast dirt on art and learning—precious worlds of hope—is anger, not neutrality.) But without detachment it's impossible to arrive at knowledge of the ways in which the new stories—rags-to-riches replacements—shore up the basic mythology of classlessness.

At the center of this mythology stands a familiar binary opposition—appearance versus reality (hierarchy as the appearance, openness as the reality). Questers advance from blindness (the delusion that class matters) to light (recognition that class is immaterial). And stories increasingly stress the rewards of downward mobility and the wisdom of redefining success (for example: success means realizing the true worth of one's present life).

As noted earlier, continuities exist between late twentieth century modes of upending and tales told generations ago. (Mark Twain taught the late nineteenth century to jeer at rich culture vultures; the classic film presentation of the rich as unenviably daffy and incompetent was *My Man Godfrey* [1936]). It's also worth noting the long line of media comedy—stretching from *Amos and Andy* through *All in the Family* and *Beverly Hillbillies* to *Sanford and Son*—that dramatizes minority and working class figures as butts, fools, or racists. It, too, contributes to the pop mythology of class-lessness, by establishing that people who don't belong to the middle are freaks. Working class characters who are portrayed as possessing normal feelings and ordinary intelligence nec-essarily pose a challenge to the myth of homogeneity, hinting at the existence of a significant social otherness. Working class characters who call their own sons-in-law "Meathead" and virtually never deviate into sense evoke no significant oth-erness. Closer to monsters than to members of any existing social class, Archie Bunkers and Homer Simpsons qualify as examples of—in sociologese—the marginalization of differ-ence. They're as insubstantial, in human terms, as an American pollster's "middle class."

Subtler, more complex themes than that of appearance versus reality figure in the media address to class (they lie directly ahead), but all are nourished by (and contiguous with) the concept of class as make-believe—a mirage incap-able of gulling the truly smart and good. The bread-and-butter fables of "classless" society are increasingly about victories over (rather than of) ambition; the point driven home is that, where change is swift and unceasing, there can be no "up" worth coveting and no "down" that lasts. What there is, in-stead, is a fantasy of omnipresence—a dream of mastering the flux through one's own nimble variousness and multi-plicity.

• *Chapter 5* •

THE OMNI SYNDROME

*E*ntering Beverly Hills, the airport limo turns onto a flower-islanded drive. Through the windows passengers glimpse tourists on the sidewalk—a trio, two grownups and a child, backs to the road, peering up at a mansion. They're completely motionless, separated from the multi-million-dollar place by a hedge and an expanse of lawn and planting. The mother holds the child's hand while Dad takes a snapshot of house and grounds.

A second glance pulls the rug out. The tourist figures aren't real—they're a lifesized, bronze work of sculpture.

The sculptor, J. Seward Johnson, Jr., has produced half a gross of these *trompe l'oeil* "narrative works" (featured in private collections here and abroad as well as at Rockefeller Center and the World Trade Center in New York and Queen Elizabeth Park in Vancouver). Pieces are cast in editions usually of seven (each casting is "personalized" for the purchaser, and the current catalog price for "Sightseeing" is $150,000, F.O.B. the artist's atelier in Trenton, New Jersey). Buying such a work is no momentous step for someone rich—nothing as demanding or expensive as acquiring a Maillol or Lipschitz. But Seward Johnson, millionaire grandson of a founder of Johnson & Johnson, has competitors among contemporary sculptors and has suffered critical deprecation, hence choosing his work is a significant decision. Owners who set "Sightseeing" at the edge of their lawn, staging a mini-masque with real property and passersby as masquers, are (in the cliché) making a statement.

By intention it's a charming statement. We see you, is the amiable message. We, the owners, may seem distant but never mind, we know what's going on out there. People stop, stare, gawk, take pictures—and why not? It's a free country. Gawking is enjoyable and being gawked at isn't so bad, either. Have a nice day.

Studied at close hand, the expressions worn by the bronze tourists communicate wonder at the splendor of the house at which they gaze; one might speculate that, in accepting the expressions as "realistic," buyers of the work find wonder appropriate, and even imagine it from inside, experiencing vicariously the fascination of the pinched with the prosperous. By decorating their grounds with a personalized version of "Sightseeing," they soften and humanize the space stretching between them and real-life strangers who contemplate them from afar. No pretended toplofty ignoring of the uninvited, no resentment at "invasions of privacy," no snub. And if the statue is a way of winking at other rich folk who are subject, like the purchasers of "Sightseeing," to sightseers' attentions, it's also a way of claiming modest access to the generality with whom one hasn't much in common.

Creating, shaping, and nourishing this taste for access is hardly the principal business of American sculptors; it is, on the other hand, a major mass media enterprise that involves cooperation with national political leaders, and that over the years has had significant impact on "classless" sensibility. The taste may blossom into casual fantasies of multiple identity; normally it's manifested simply as relish of brief, imaginary, undemanding closings of the gap between self and others. When the taste is slaked, pecking orders seem less confining and inhibiting; temporary diversification of social identity feels both possible and virtuous. As a sprightly citizen-democrat I'm not locked into my status but am at ease (in my fancy) with people differently situated. Matters would be otherwise if European-style class distinctions were with us. But happily they've been done away with—seen through, replaced. If I choose, I can appropriate other people's experience, exploring it sportively in an as-if mode.

These gently protean impulses of mine clothe themselves differently in accordance with where I live (politics, commerce, the world of entertainment), and stimulate a myriad of responses—gaiety, affection, admiration, surprise. (Who would have thought that I knew *them*, or that they knew me? Who would have thought that someone who ordinarily behaves as I do can also behave thus?) Always the primary effect is a freshening of the sense of social freedom; always I'm assured that reaching out and touching them is within my range.

Top dogs in commerce and industry—leaders vested with option-fat salaries, personal jets, retreats in Aspen and St. John—have immemorially presented themselves as interchangeable with guys and gals on the line. "I'm out in my shirtsleeves, where the action is," says the CEO of a giant newspaper conglomerate. "I'm as comfortable rewriting a headline as I am making a corporate acquisition." "I was their pal," says Lee Iacocca, remembering his relations with "union guys" in his autobiography. "They embraced me." "I'm a biker," said Malcolm Forbes. And spokesmen for Old Families have tended to claim that they, too, qualify as exemplars of social range. "The beneficiaries of the Old Money curriculum," writes Nelson Aldrich in *Old Money* (1988), "come into a social life in which they can enjoy the freedom and mobility of middle-class social life, the stability of the social life of the poor, or some combination of the two, as they wish."

But mass entertainment has democratized relaxed, downward access, proposing it as a life-possibility for nearly all, even contriving special forms to accommodate it—the celebrity cameo appearance, for one. Mysteriously stars or public figures appear at the doors of average American sitcom families; mysteriously they "know," in the manner of neighbors, one or another family member and are embraced as pals. Sammy Davis, Jr. shows himself to be acquainted with Edith Bunker during his conversation, in yesteryear, with Archie Bunker in the latter's living room, on *All in the Family*; Nancy Reagan knows everyone on *Diff'rent Strokes*. The drop-in can be a oneshot joke (Richard Nixon crying "Sock It to Me!" on *Laugh-In*) or a one-inning stint (Ronald Reagan in the NBC booth at the 1989 All Star game). Often, though, it's worked up as a go-along bit throughout an entire episode, as in a *Bob Newhart Show* featuring a cameo by Johnny Carson.

Initially this script scoffs at access as nutty wishfulness. Newhart, playing the part of a New Yorker turned Vermont innkeeper, is discovered at his desk paying bills. Enter three unkempt, redneck brothers, regulars on the show—Larry, Daryl, and Daryl—to whom Newhart is stiffly courteous (the noblesse oblige of displaced urban man). Learning that Bob

THE OMNI SYNDROME • 77

Newhart is at this moment writing a check for his gas bill, Larry expresses puzzlement. He explains that "Johnny Carson pays our gas bill." Skepticism, defensiveness, and showbiz allusions follow. "It seems farfetched," says Bob. "I don't think Bob believes us," says Larry. Carson has time to pay Larry's bills, says Tom Poston, handyman, because "he does have his Monday nights off."

Irritated by Newhart's doubt and disdain, the rednecks at length explode. "We've got better things to do than stand around and be humored," says Larry. The three exit, resolved to produce proof.

Twice they return, first to offer up a shoebox filled with gas company invoices (Newhart pulls out a bill, reads the words scribbled on it—"This bill was paid by Johnny Carson"—and is abruptly dismissive), later to bring on Carson himself, for his cameo. "You're the Yahoo who called my friend Larry a liar," says the *Tonight Show* host to Newhart in pretended anger. "You know what irks me about you? All you ever do is take take take. Why don't you give once in a while? Cheap cheap cheap cheap." Newhart sags in defeat: "It isn't easy being me."

Laughter. Pleasures of access all around. Now this.

More ambitious sitcoms treat the themes of interchange-ability and access contrapuntally. Major characters step from above to below, socially, while supporting players do the opposite. In the sitcom called *Designing Women*, Julia and Suzanne Sugarbaker (sisters), Mary Jo Shively, and Charlene run a flourishing decorating business. Finely groomed and coiffed figures of brio and wit, they—and their gleaming showroom-office—epitomize upscale, imperial middle luxury and style.

But the partners are sparklingly mobile. In one segment

a strike is called in the textile plant from which they're buying curtain material for a motel decorating job, and their own office is picketed. At first the four women respond differently to the event, with the show's comic butt—Suzanne—showing hostility to the strikers. Soon, though, the women come down firmly against the manufacturer (and against their own interests as entrepreneurs); they enter smoothly into the strikers' lives. Their office produces coffee and muffins for the picketers, one of whom has hurled tomatoes at their own door. Visiting the struck curtain factory, the designers sit and work at machines usually run by Asian-American seamstresses, and are troubled by the awkwardness of the postures the machines require of those tending them. After earnest talk with a worker who happens upon them in the plant, they renounce their contract to decorate the motel, proclaiming full solidarity with the strike. "We are all Labor," cries elegant Julia Sugarbaker.

Back at the showroom, in tonight's subplot, Anthony, the designers' engaging, black, ex-con van driver, is displaying social fluency matching that of his chic employers. Service managers at the garage that's fixing Mary Jo Shively's car have been jerking her around. Seeking satisfaction for Shively, speaking in her voice on the phone to a mechanic at the garage (black ex-con male mimics genteel white female entrepreneur), Anthony talks knowledgeably about loose rocker arms and faulty pistons. Impressed, the mechanic at the other end of the line asks Anthony for a date.

Nor are we done: at the show's end, learning of new turpitude on the part of the garage, the designers-turned-strikers recast themselves yet again, as marching activists. Their exquisitely manicured hands take up arms (fruit suitable for defacing plate glass garage windows), and the four women head for the door; as we go to commercial we hear the start of a Sixties-style chant: FREE THE SHIVELY VOLVO.

Sitcoms are comedy, needless to say. But they shuttle handily from chuckles to heartfeltness and are arranged to permit easy intercourse between the sophisticated and naive. Belief and unbelief rub shoulders in the audience as on the set; scripts and performers represent many factions—cynics, faithful, "socially concerned." Costume and situation announce that "We are all Labor!" is an absurdity. But vehemence of voice and perfervid expression of sympathy for the abused warn against dismissing the cry. Similar doubleness attends the Carson cameo show. Informed showbiz talk counters, for the pseudo-worldly, the goody premise that rube-loving celebrities abound, but Newhart's comeuppance establishes, for the ingenuous, that it's a mistake to believe chaps in overalls aren't good enough to be pals with Johnny Carson. Implicit in the laughlines is a blueprint of an idealized social scene—relaxed, brotherly, fluid, open.

One reason that the scene plays is that it has ties to imperial middle assumptions about personal variousness—to the belief, that is, that the middle is almost limitlessly encompassing, denied intimacy with none but society's farthest out fringes (rapists, child abusers, surrogate mothers). Story lines and comic bits echo and instill confidence that each has access to all—the omni syndrome—and that social distance is unreal. Gaps between us and them close upon personal command. Those whom I wish to salute and know, I know (no impediment); those whom I desire briefly to become, I briefly become.

The omni idea drives Peace Corps and Vista volunteers by the thousands to darkest Africa and neediest Appalachia. It's sent millions of Americans "on the road," hitchhiking after the grail of Experience, and it's aroused appetites, among the sedentary urban and suburban middle-aged, for rough-tough, raw-country vehicles called Broncos. Under its sway college students from the north traveled south to work in Freedom Schools and voter registration projects, and one writer "passed" as black for the purpose of learning the race story "from inside." Bemused by the mystique of access—of in-touchness with "all walks of life"—rich and middling-rich finagle summer jobs for their children on road crews or as muck-out hands in racing stables. A Harvard Rockefeller Scholar reports that, on her travels, she "cut vegetables in the kitchen of an Irish castle and took a course in the New Hampshire woods in emergency medicine where, among other things, [she] learned to set a broken femur with a ski pole." Heroin addicts do turns as stand-up comics in Manhattan parks and are reviewed in *The Village Voice*; a Renaissance scholar/university president becomes baseball commissioner; an ex-President of the United States works as a carpenter in a Habitat housing project; Mose T., a primitive artist in red-clay Alabama is snatched off to the National Gallery to pose beside Mrs. Reagan. Asked why she "lives in jeans," the pop singer k. d. lang responds that: "I like to pretend I'm a farmer and sort of dress for chores. Always ready to feed the cows, drive the tractor, fix the truck."

It's the omni vision, not ambition alone, that propels black kids from inner city homes and pleasures to Fresh Air Camps and whitey prep schools and investment house training programs. It's the omni vision that inspires Tina Fredrick's praise of Andy Warhol as the Everything Man ("he goes out and he registers everything and he does that everything and he becomes everything. The everything man"). And it's the same vision—an idea of visiting another life, a life of art, a life above, a life below—that fills writing classes the country over with working class whites, and creates "unions" of auto-worker-gospel singers all through the South, and encourages thousands of rock groups to make demo records in studios, and turns numberless heirs into gentleman-farmers. Omni plays, in short, because it speaks in the U.S.A. to universal desire ("knowing one's way around") and universal fear (being "limited"); each of its multifarious forms is a version of the American *Pilgrim's Progress*.

In the media as in real life three omni styles predominate: career, rhetorical, and political. Career omnis proliferate everywhere from *60 Minutes* segments to local paper feature pages, embracing banker-cellists, stockbroker-heavyweights, thespian-racecar drivers (or thespian mayors and chief executives). But in the third quarter of the twentieth century the best-known career omni in America was, of course, George Plimpton, Harvard-educated son of patrician New England, whose omni picaresques entertained millions of *Sports Illustrated* readers. Genial bonhomie marks Plimpton's encounters with pro baseball and football players, golfers, pugilists, and others, and the material with which he works varies little from story to story. Initially there's a sketch of the writer's background (to define obstacles that aliens unschooled in omni faith might assume would hamper Plimpton's effort to secure access to the déclassé). The obstacles include the writer's "eastern seaboard cosmopolitan accent" (the players "thought [it] was 'British' "), the writer's ineptness at swearing (never having heard the key terms at home), the writer's interest in judging athletes' comparative levels of intelligence ("The four years of college rub off [on football players]. The average intelligence has got to be higher—certainly higher than in baseball)."

On occasion, sketching background, Plimpton goes so far as to remember moments in his past that would seem to set absolutely unbridgable social distance between him and, say, the latest Dominican lad to scratch his way to the majors. At Yankee Stadium, about to throw his first pitch to a lineup of all-star batters that includes Willie Mays (Mays flies out), Plimpton recalls that the last ball game in which he played occurred in a Loire Valley meadow belonging to the Château of Maillebois. The participants included the lunch guests, the chateau owner, and a "young countess playing in bare feet"; at game's end "when we walked up through the dusk there were lights burning in one of the chateau towers."

After the sketch of social background the writer directly confronts—and overturns—skepticism about the ability of an omni patrician to close vast social gulfs. Sometimes the evidence consists of accounts of gestures by players attesting to the patrician's power to ingratiate himself. (The Detroit Lions would "come around to my room and they'd ask if I wanted to come into town. They had begun to accept me as one of them.") In other works the author shows us, teasingly, his ability to bring off a self-transformation by observing the manners of pro athletes; arriving at an inventory of what he takes to be the basic elements of mulish mindlessness, he mimics them comically, one by one. In *Out of My League* he writes that "My voice [at Yankee Stadium] took on a vague, tough timbre—somewhat Southern-cracker in tone—and the few sentences I spoke were cryptic yet muffled; I created a strange, sloping, farmer's walk; once I found myself leaning forward on my knee, spiked shoe up on the batting-cage wheel, chin cupped in hand, squinting darkly toward center field like a brooding manager; I was sorely tempted to try a stick of gum, despite my dislike of the stuff, in order to get the jaws moving professionally. Sometimes I just moved the jaws anyway, chewing on the corner of the tongue."

The climax of each Plimpton comedy entails reversal. The omni patrician who salutes and masters from above in his cameo is himself saluted and mastered from below. A light-heavyweight champ recognizes Plimpton's pugilistic incompetence and taps him restrainedly with his gloved fist, merely bloodying his nose. A pitching coach on the bench recognizes that Plimpton has reached a state of exhaustion and helps him from the mound. A defensive line, grasping his vulnerability, dumps him—the aspiring rookie quarterback—relatively gently on his butt. The circle of knowledge closes; the career-omni knower is known; the happy access of all to all is again affirmed.

Rhetorical omni speaks solely to the lettered and involves takeover by trope. Access becomes a verbal conceit; what is distinctive in the experience of a socially distant other is rendered homogeneous—by a figure of speech—with what is ordinary in me; radically different kinds of experience are linked, in *concordia discors*, as interchangeable. As elsewhere in the omni media scene, the tone is playfully protective and the touch soothingly light.

One example of the mode is found in George W. S. Trow's *Within the Context of No Context* (1981), in an essay introducing the recording impresario Jerry Wexler. The essay describes as follows Wexler's contribution to the success of a famous soul singer:

> Aretha Franklin had recorded for a number of years for Columbia, where her genius had been recognized but where no material appropriate to her genius had been

given her. In her first session at Atlantic, Jerry Wexler gave her a song called "I Never Loved a Man the Way I Love You." This song (rougher, more rural, more Southern, more like the simple blues, but not less "arranged" than the songs she had recorded for Columbia) established a voice for her and a presence in the commercial marketplace. Later songs confirmed her reputation as the most significant black voice of the time and *Jerry Wexler's reputation as the most significant white man making black music.* [Emphasis added]

Left motherless at six, Aretha Franklin—the artist in question—was raised by her father, a singer-preacher with a "reputation as a ladies' man." She struggled to win his approval ("she would do anything to please him," said her first manager), sang in his gospel show at age five, became a regular in his road troupe at fourteen (for blacks in the Fifties traveling was an education in hate). Her first child was born when she was fifteen, her second when she was seventeen. Her first husband beat her in public. The song called "I Never Loved a Man" emerged at the height of the black struggle for civil rights, and at least one critic has observed, in response to the intensity of the performance, that Aretha Franklin transformed it from a torch song into a cry for political freedom. The force of a lifetime's experience of betrayal, oppression, and helpless attachment resounds in its phrases as Franklin molds them, as does the influence of a remarkable musical training. (Ms. Franklin's tutors in gospel music included Mahalia Jackson as well as her father, and she had numerous jazz masters.) She herself produced the arrangement for "I Never Loved a Man," working together determinedly with a quartet of topnotch studio musicians. ("It took some real thought," one of the musicians later recalled in an interview with Peter Guralnick quoted in Guralnick's *Sweet Soul Music* (1986). "There wasn't anybody around [except Aretha] that could play it.")

Obviously the impresario described in the article as a "maker of black music" makes black music by promoting it, not by playing or singing. But speaking of him as a musicmaker closes the distance between singer and promoter. There's an allusion to the presumed dependence of black music on sympathetic white makers, and also a hint that the parity between Franklin and Wexler is rooted in intimacy. (*We know them better than they know themselves.*) The linkage has a democratic flavor ("Democracy," said John Dewey, "is conjoint communicated experience"), as well as a component of selfless generosity (a white man makes black music for the benefit of blacks).

But the primary rhetorical project is to equate Wexler's "giving her a song" with Aretha Franklin's giving voice to the troubled longings—the full response to life—of an entire people. The agency of an omni pun (on "making") banishes difference so that an orderly, sanitized world of personnel, logistics, and bottom lines can be evoked as perfectly continuous with Aretha Franklin's world—privy to pain and chaos, deeply inward with a young artist's fury, exultation, capacity for extraordinarily self-transcending emotion, and achievement of sounds commensurate with that knowledge.

Political omni is best represented currently in the behavior of and media reporting on President George Bush. The style is low key. When citing evidence of personal or familial variousness—drawing attention, for instance, to the Hispanic babies in a flock of his largely WASP grandchildren, or analogizing the search for his roots in the Netherlands to Alex Haley's search for his roots in Africa—the President and those who cover him are never windy. (A single quoted phrase— "the little brown ones over there"—makes the point.) Neither comparisons nor autobiographical reflections accompany the President's expressions of enthusiasm for recreations and entertainments associated with class levels remote from his own. The tennis-playing, fly-fishing, quail-hunting Skull and Bones Yalie shows his spirit of access instead of telling it, enjoying pork rinds and Tabasco, adding a horseshoe-pitching court to the White House grounds, eating popcorn at the movies, faithfully tuning to the country music show called *Hee-Haw*, falling asleep nightly to bedside tapes of Crystal Gayle and Loretta Lynn, entertaining Tammy Faye Bakker at lunch. And each detail dramatizing his social range—the old Ivy New England past, the high-rolling Texas future—wins space and punditry in the papers.

In addition to career, rhetorical, and political omni, several lesser, media-based and developed styles bid for notice, and among them *performer-omni*—the ancient art of impersonation adapted to the needs and tempo of post-industrial life—ranks as most piquant. Virtuosi in this style tear at breakneck rates through the social landscape, sampling class, ethnic, occupational idioms and voices, assuming characters (addict, star, pedant, politico, Russian, French, English, Chinese) and dropping them at almost the instant they're suggested, dramatizing the endless, hilarious possibilities of counterfeit being. The style is hyper, never low key; it drives itself fiercely toward ever more astonishing feats of whirlwind inclusiveness; it imagines the whole of its audience as material. "People are my high," shouts the comic Robin Williams, grandmaster of performer omni. "I'd like the audience to lie down on the mirror right now. I want to snort you people."

Williams and his peers ratchet up the omni fantasy to levels remote from those attainable in conventional, non-theatrical settings; their wit, magic, and astonishing charm make ordinary omni turns—George Bush breaking bread with Tammy Faye Bakker, a millionaire setting bronze sightseers on his lawn—seem humdrum if not labored. But the fundamentals of the omni pursuit remain constant across the spectrum regardless of the chosen styles or native gifts of the players. The name of the game is access; the unvarying assumption is that each can easily know all.

There are risks in the omni culture, especially for politicians. The heady freedom that permits leaders to choose social selves in accordance with situation and taste can lead to personality fractionation—even memory loss. Washington doesn't need "Harvard Yard's boutique"—"a philosophical cult"—trying to run the country, said candidate George Bush, scorning his Harvard-educated opponent's softness toward namby-pamby Cambridge intellectuals. The idiom was that of a standard Ivy League baiter who possesses no direct knowledge of the real defects or real virtues of the institutions disparaged. Yet George Bush, the Ivy-baiter, in other contexts often details loving memories of his own New Haven days. Access on this order—access that permits the boundaries of a social identity to be redrawn daily—can have moral consequences. (Now the high road, now the low, now the smear, now the shocked disavowal of intent to harm, and always a troubling delight in image-switching: "This guy they used to call timid," said the President, with satisfaction, after the Panama invasion, "is now a macho man.")

What's more, confusion traceable to the political omni style can infect entire households. The President-Elect's wife, for her part, found it desirable during Inauguration Week, when she appeared at a Republican Women's luncheon wearing an expensive designer suit, to disavow the access to the *haut monde* implicit in the choice of the garment. On the speaker's platform Mrs. Bush mockingly displayed the jacket's tailoring and lining: "Please notice . . . the designers' clothes," said the First Lady. "And remember. You may never see it again." Claiming membership in the plain people (clients of Lands' End and Talbots), erasing ownership of a five million dollar summer estate and substantial trust funds, presenting sensible frugality and fear of waste as norms for a family accustomed for decades to spending hundreds of thousands a year—as surely as Ivy-baiting by an Ivy, these actions can set a mind on the road to fractionation and amnesia.

Or, at the minimum, toward silliness—another risk of political omni. A discussion, by the First Lady, of meals and protocol begins purposefully. "You try to make [a state dinner] interesting," Mrs. Bush observes. "You try to get a cross section." But at once the tone changes, earnestness is whisked away, and yesterday's wimp factor is reactivated. "George comes up with the most marvelous mix and makes it much more fun. I always giggle over the guest list George comes up with."

The pursuit of political omni (earlier ages spoke of it as attempting to be "all things to all men") has a long history in the "classless" state—but its status remains shaky: it could be compromised by a giggle.

More generally, there's the problem of bad faith. Behavior implying that one would like to stand closer to a distant group—gestures that communicate awareness of, and interest in, socially remote others—can be read gratefully and believingly by the distant; discovery that the gestures are hollow induces the misanthropy of the suckered. In *Paper Lion* (1966) George Plimpton reported himself astonished to learn that various team members read his gestures as his substance, believed him to be a genuinely committed presence among them—and were infuriated on catching whiffs of his detachment. During a Detroit-Cleveland game, Plimpton, in uniform on the bench, turned away once from the action to gaze at a pretty cheerleader, whereupon the pro next to him, enraged, struck him hard on the shoulder pads: " 'Keep your mind on the game,' he said. I began to grin at him, thinking he wasn't serious, but he was furious. 'What do you mean looking behind you like that? What's going on that concerns you is in *front* of you.' His voice shook, he was so angry. 'Concentrate,' he said. 'Concentrate all the time on that game out there.' "

The player's confusion was partly the result of naïveté *cum* competitive frenzy—partly but not wholly. Both his fury and Plimpton's bewildered response testify that, although exposure to omni styles is unceasing because of the media, people know little about the operation and effects of those styles, or about their potential, in a culture determined to deny the existence of social differences, for causing painful disillusionment. Intention is immaterial; playacted intimacy often deceives. Exploiting vast electronic resources, the would-be "man of the people"—the political omni fond both of strategic gestures of access and of the language of kindness—persuades millions of his earnest concern for the people's needs; the realization that these are mere gestures —that, like Plimpton, the man of the people is only putatively on the bench of gritty life—weakens an already frail public trust in governance.

Another problem arising from the media-promoted omni syndrome is that of reductiveness. The impulse to reach out to those differently situated needs to be accompanied by clarity about the strength and weight of the particulars of experience that define substantive human identity, otherwise a process of trivialization is set in course. But most omni rhetoric shrugs off those particulars—as when it likens the achievements of Jerry Wexler, a rich, white corporate executive, to that of Aretha Franklin, a black artist reared in torment, thereby disconnecting knowledge from living. ("Only so much do I know," said Emerson, "as I have lived.") In the name of pseudo-fraternity the style sports with differences of life experience and situation, and implicitly lodges a claim that the theory and practice of access is the same at the bottom as at the top. The result is a mist of unreality.

It should be acknowledged, in fairness, that pop entertainment does introduce corrective realism on occasion. A movie hero or heroine destined to play out an omni fantasy—to soar above all class obstructions—is checked for an instant. Space is made in which an audience can grasp the connection between levels of knowledge and levels of privilege. A person reached toward from above or below is seen to possess inner, mysterious resources (or limits) about which someone differently placed can have no inkling, and cannot conceivably lay claim.

Such a moment (from above to below) occurs in the film *Working Girl*. The character played by Melanie Griffith is an ambitious nobody in a word-processing pool; she struggles to sterilize her accent in speech classes, snatches up any unconsidered trifle of information about dressing for success, labors hard to master the configurations of data out of which "investment analysts" like her aristo boss construct opinions that create "hot stocks." She progresses. Her boss provides her with useful tips on costume and hairstyle, finds merit in a line of reasoning Melanie develops concerning a prospective merger, talks warmly (and deceitfully) to Melanie about "trust." Possibility beckons and it's seized; before the end Melanie stands as an omni triumph—an Executive installed in an office of her own, elevated to the ranks of onetime gofers who know at last what it's like to be a sender.

But for an instant there *is* a check. Following orders, Melanie as secretarial underling books her boss, played by Sigourney Weaver, into a chalet for a ski weekend. She's helping Sigourney fasten her new ski boots in the office when she's asked where in the chalet the room is located. Melanie doesn't know; Sigourney dials the resort and at once a flood of flawless German fills the room. The camera angle shows us Melanie's awe; we gaze up with her (from the glossy white boots that she, as footman, is buckling) to this animated, magical Ivy-educated master/mistress of the world, self-transformed into Europe, performing in another language, demonstrating casually that bottom dogs have no exact knowledge of what lies between them and their ideal, that top dogs possess secret skills that they can conceal with ease forever (or all at once ravishingly display)—skills nobody learns overnight, as in charm class, or by changing hairstyles ... skills traceable to uncounted indulgent hours of tutoring, study, and travel.

The moment is beautifully played; the seconds stretch on; the bottom dog's eyes widen; a frightening truth dawns. If a talent so mesmerizing—this poured-forth foreign self— can be invisible until now, can be hidden so effortlessly, must there not be others equally well concealed? Is it not likely that this dream of mine—this hunger to be her—is impossible? What unimaginable barriers stand between me and my desire?

But in the culture of the omni syndrome—as in this

movie, minutes later—the answer to such questions is, of course: No real barriers, none. "Be all you can be" means, at the bottom as at the top, "Be whatever you wish," fear no obstacle, see no obstacle, there are no obstacles; life (in the imperial middle) is an omni orgy. Others aren't other, one knows them as well as one knows oneself, one takes their place in a trice. This buoyant, utterly unfounded confidence that knowledge of all but the most remote others flows like water from the tap qualifies, perhaps, as the most dubious aspect of the omni syndrome. Caught up in the illusion, the middle glides in fancy on channels never closed; possessing little experience of circumscription and no appetite for discomfiture by guilt, it's persuaded, at some level, of the comparative universality of its own unboundedness. Facts of difference (mere externals) are played down, and the possibility of instant intimacy with people and situations as yet unencountered is played up; gulfs separating groups are *known* to be quickly bridged by complaisant words and gestures ("kinder," "gentler").

And the result is a pervasive top-down perspective that's troublingly all-knowing both for and about others. What is it that the black man wants? Why, says a sitting Secretary of Agriculture, "Coloreds only want three things. First, a tight pussy; second, loose shoes; and, third, a warm place to shit." Why is the all-black, Oliver North jury taking so long to reach a verdict? Why, says Arthur Liman, Chief Counsel to the Senate Select Committee, answering a reporter's questions at an elegant ball, They're enjoying the hotel. "If they can send the corrections officer for a pack of cigarets—that's high living." The others (as media-represented) seem this accessible to interpretation: fully readable and available, yielding the whole of themselves instantly to whatever perfunctory glance turns their way—as open and eager for interrogation, appropria-

tion, and "understanding" as the defenseless wretched inter-
viewed by Donahue and Oprah Winfrey.

Mimics who, in the performer omni style, reduce other
human beings to a coke hit or blast—"I'd like the audience
to lie down on the mirror right now"—define what is, for
them, a functional vision. For stars people are fans, the fuel
of elation—a collective airy powder providing pleasing illusions of control and command. But for human relations in a
real world—as for politics and social policy—this vision of
others is less functional. Like the high of the "marvelous mix,"
it eats away sincerity and authenticity; under its influence
guest-list makers go wilding but knowledge of others goes
blank. And it is the essential vision of the omni culture. In
amending or replacing rags-to-riches tales, the media can be
seen as merely changing the key of the old anthems of classlessness. In promoting democratic omnipresence as a value,
the media venture a step further, toward the refashioning of
social psychology, and the consequences are not benign. The
nature of the elements that constitute selves—fragments of
thought, feeling, attitude, memory—ceases to be understood;
skills and arts essential to patient ordering and interpretation
of differences rust unpracticed; the heavy substance of social
being is atomized. Snorting others, omni-syndromers grow
weightless themselves.

• *Chapter 6* •

CLASS COVERUP: THREE MASKING LANGUAGES

*T*he third major media contribution to the "classless" society is the development of substitutes for the traditional language of class. Improvisation and minor modifications of technical vocabularies favored by social scientists are the principal features of the substitute languages. And because conflicting constituencies are served, ambiguity is close to their essence. The larger constituency is composed, obviously, of those who decently or evasively find class talk abhorrent; the smaller constituency is composed of those for whom class talk serves as a means of releasing hostility to "inferiors," usually blacks and minorities, sometimes Jews, on occasion tradespeople, counterworkers, "help." The substitute languages serve two ends. First they enable the larger constituency to draw distinctions without employing offensive terms—terms that announce flat-out the existence of a class society. Second, they open up a resource bank of innuendo enabling those impatient with cant about equality to come a step closer to candor. For different reasons both constituencies retreat from explicitness, hence a certain sly delicacy marks the languages in question; their operations come clear only through perusal of examples.

A Surrogate Uterus

Diagnostic languages now conventional in forensic medicine and psychology are taken up eagerly by the press in daily reporting and opinion columns. Class differences are redefined as psychogenic differences, and the powers of the professional are thereby augmented; confidence in non-technical interpretations of behavior is weakened, and the gap between the center and the fringes is widened.

Notable examples of the language in action turned up in coverage of the trial of Mary Beth Whitehead, mother of "Baby M." A question frequently posed as the case developed was: "What kind of woman would consent to bear and sell her child?" The answers from a team of expert psychologists were reported in detail. Mrs. Whitehead was described as "impulsive, egocentric, self-dramatic, manipulative and exploitative." One member of the team averred that she suffered from a "schizotypal personality disorder." A world-famous authority, Dr. Lee Salk, agreed with the team view and gave it as his opinion that the defendant's ailment was a "mixed personality disorder," and that she was "immature, exhibitionistic, and histrionic." Salk testified further that, under the circumstances, he did not see that "there were any 'parental rights' "; Mrs. Whitehead was "a surrogate uterus"—the phrase made headlines—"and not a surrogate mother."

The defense effort at countering the experts failed, and the Court awarded custody of the child to William and Betsy Stern (the couple who had retained the "surrogate uterus"), declaring that "the parental rights of the defendant, Mary Beth Whitehead, are terminated." (A subsequent New Jersey Supreme Court decision restored Mrs. Whitehead's parental rights of visitation but left standing the custody decision.)

The issue of class did in fact surface at intervals during Mrs. Whitehead's trial. The prosecution contrasted the occupations, educational levels, and resources of the Sterns with those of the Whiteheads. (Mr. Whitehead was a garbageman and truckdriver; once, when briefly separated from him, Mrs. Whitehead worked as a barroom dancer; William Stern is a biochemist and Betsy Stern is a pediatrician.) The prosecution listed Mr. Whitehead's loss of a job among the reasons that custody of the baby should not be awarded to him and his wife. Mrs. Whitehead's lawyer, for his part, spoke of class exploitation in his summation: "What we are witnessing," he declared, "and what we can predict will happen, is that one class of Americans will exploit another class. And it will always be the wife of the sanitation worker who must bear the children for the pediatrician."

The media reported this summation, with its theme that life is harder for the poor than for the rich. But the important and publicly influential commitment had already been made —to the language of science that placed Mrs. Whitehead close either to derangement or to the man-machine interface. Might matters have gone differently had an interpretive language of class been available? Could the media, through "investigative reporting"—or a defense attorney not content to stop at complaints about injustice and unequal economic means—have developed, for the public, a better level of understanding? Free to speak the full language of class—as distinguished from cant about the sorrows of the poor—might they have managed to restore Mrs. Whitehead to the human community?

Very likely. Competent, sympathetic inquiry into the background of the woman's behavior—her motivation, misinformation, naïveté, sense of self—could easily have rendered comprehensible those actions that the approved masking language rendered bizarre. The defendant was in court because she had broken her contract with the Sterns and kidnapped her baby. The prosecution explained her offense by presenting her as mentally aberrant or ill. The defense explained it by presenting her as a victim of social injustice. Both presentations concealed the realities that bore most powerfully on her actions. Mrs. Whitehead broke her contract because she learned, long after signing it, that it required her to commit deeds that were beyond her capacity. She broke faith—in human, non-legal terms—with the Sterns because she came to realize (again, long after agreeing to help them) that the couple thought of her as their employee. Her reactions were rooted in her class background and could not be understood, whether in their legal or human dimensions, except in relation to that background.

The question "What kind of woman would bear and sell her child?" may or may not have been a fair question. The fair answer, as it emerged, was: A woman not strikingly different from any other in her circumstance; a woman who is one of us.*

---

*Materials supporting that answer are found in Mrs. Whitehead's autobiography—
A Mother's Story (1989). As an attempt at self-defense and a work written with the aid of a freelance writer, the book is suspect—but in fact there is little cunning contrivance in its pages. The author and her collaborator, Loretta Schwartz-Nobel, have no interest in or bent for elucidating class factors influencing behavior; their touching and credible story misses many opportunities that other, more manipulative authors would have seized—with perfect justification—in producing an airtight self-vindication.

Mrs. Whitehead conceived of herself as a person engaged not in a money-making venture but in helping the Sterns in a manner she had been taught to expect both of herself and others. The surrogate mother had learned early in life that meager means oblige people to sacrifice for each other— even for those to whom they are unrelated by blood. (Necessity in the form of non-existent insurance policies and fallback funds dictates the behavior.) Her mother, a single parent with eight children who was erratically employed as a beautician, had called frequently on neighbors for extended help. Mrs. Whitehead lived a portion of her own childhood with poor but generous neighbors, and she and her husband often shared the burdens of friends incapacitated by accident or other emergency, over long periods of time.*

The surrogate mother was to be paid for bearing Melissa Stern, and she knew the Sterns were financially better off than herself. But she envisaged the couple, seemingly desperate in their childlessness, threatened by a ruinous disease (Mrs. Stern's self-diagnosed multiple sclerosis,) as people in trouble, unable to cope without her. Putting the same point differently, Mrs. Whitehead read their emergency in the light of her past. She had seen people turn to others helplessly in distress, had herself been turned to previously; in her world

---

*"[Sue] needed complete care," Mrs. Whitehead writes of a neighbor injured in an accident. "She had to be fed and bathed. Her teeth had to be brushed, her nose had to be blown. She also needed someone to help take care of her two young children and take over her job in the family's swimming pool business.

"Each morning at seven I came over with [my children]. First we'd all eat breakfast together. Then I'd get the kids off to school. After that I'd dress Sue and do her housework and the scheduling and banking for the family business. Then I'd do the cooking. Rick would come over and eat dinner with us. At eight o'clock he would take my kids home to do their homework. I'd stay on until eleven and come home after getting Sue to bed.

"Even though it was a hard routine, I enjoyed helping her. It's the kind of thing I've always been best at." *A Mothers' Story*, pp. 149–150.

failure to respond was unnatural. Her class experience, together with her own individual nature, made it natural to perceive the helping side of the surrogacy as primary and the commercial side as important yet secondary.

One other class-related circumstance—the surrogate mother's ignorance of the technology of artificial insemination—appears also to have figured significantly in her action. Almost to the hour of Melissa Stern's birth, Mrs. Whitehead believed that "the procedure included implanting the woman's egg as well as the man's sperm, and that it actually enabled the infertile couple to have their own genetic child." No one in or out of authority explained to her that she herself "would be doing everything that a woman does to produce her own child, including providing half of the genetic inheritance. . . ." or that "I wasn't giving Betsy Stern *her* baby, I was giving her *my* baby."

Her ignorance could be traced to her harried parent, or to the distancing, class-related attitudes of the professionals who were caring for her, or to failures of early schooling. (An accident disfigured Mrs. Whitehead in her youth, bringing ridicule upon her in school; she dropped out at fifteen.) Levels of knowledge concerning human sexual reproduction are well known to vary from class to class, with poor information and superstition not uncommon among working class young. Mrs. Whitehead's unawareness that she had contracted to bear and sell her own child appears to have had its origin in the same class experience that molded her conviction that it was up to her to aid the pitiably vulnerable and needy Sterns. It hardly qualified as a symptom of mental illness, or marked her off from common humanness; it testified only to one dimension of her class identity.

Much more could be said to bring into focus the social

context of Mrs. Whitehead's behavior, but again full analysis of class-specific feelings and attitudes is less important than recognition that nothing resembling such analysis was put in print or given voice on the nightly news, and that, as a result, an entirely normal, giving human being was placed beyond reach of fellow feeling. The masking language—"schizotypal," "surrogate uterus," and the rest—obliterated the intricately configured attitudes, beliefs, and experiences that constituted Mrs. Whitehead's class identity and that offered access to her humanity.

The pattern is often repeated. Motives and actions unfamiliar to the imperial middle are separated by the media and others from their social grounding; behavior which, firmly set in its context, qualifies as predictable and normal, functional and adaptive, is represented as worse than freakish. Tacit proscription bans the only language truly commensurate with the task of probing connections between actions and backgrounds. And that ban opens the door to speculation that no such connections exist.

Science and law stand ready at this door, contending that diagnostic fact alone deserves trust; the lingo sounds objective (hence suitable for the media); picked up by the populace it becomes common speech. In hard-edged terms the suggestion is pressed that the fundamental sameness of human creatures is a delusion: some among us are so extraordinarily different—so exceptionally far removed from the average—that no violence is done by representing them as quasi-machines. The masking language stops only a little short of transforming social difference into species difference.

He Frightens with His Power

The most deliberate and ingenious masking of class differences occurs in the media's political discourse. It's especially frequent in treatment of subjects and areas wherein minorities are prominent, and has become a staple of coverage of the "Jackson phenomenon."

An example: during the floor demonstration that followed Jesse Jackson's speech at the last Democratic convention, Dan Rather and Walter Cronkite shared their reactions with viewers. Rather considered the nation fortunate that Jackson spoke from inside an official arena: "The thought keeps coming to mind that not only is the Democratic Party, but perhaps the country, is lucky to have a Jesse Jackson who is within the system, wants to participate in the mainstream system. . . ." Cronkite acknowledged both the power of the Jackson address and the man's significance as spokesperson for the "disenfranchised." But he added: "I think he is so powerful, however, that perhaps he frightens some people with his power. We, some of us who are perhaps a little older, Eric [Sevareid] and I, would, I guess, count ourselves among those individuals. [We] watched the rise of people who seemed to be speaking for the underprivileged for a long period of time, and then after, when power came, things went awry."

In this instance class differences are masked as differences in cultural experience and heritage, and in commitment to democratic values. An implicit contrast is drawn between members of minorities emerging from obscurity to claim a share of power and members of the imperial middle accustomed to possessing power. The initial language is social (the "disenfranchised" and the "underprivileged" versus "we" and "us"). But the terms change swiftly, and the final contrast reduces the difference in question to one between people who can be trusted to uphold the nation's political traditions and norms, and people likely to be duped into abandoning them.

Walter Cronkite's intent wasn't to smear Jacksonites as embryonic young Fascists. His cautious, tentative tone showed him to be aware that, at a moment when everyone (including the comparative youngster in the booth with him) was caught up in enthusiasm, and when the focus of good feeling was a member of a minority once excluded from the process, dour reflections were clearly out of key. Thanks to the "McGovern rules," the floor of the Democratic Convention had been opened to people new to the process—blacks, Hispanics, women.... They were aroused and the force of their feeling for their leader swelled and surged, reaching into the broadcast booth itself. Gloom and foreboding were plainly out of keeping with such excitement.

Still, the commentator seems to have told himself, there was reason for unease—occasion for stern if gentle reminders. He and his colleague Sevareid remembered a time when demagoguery became terror. Masses of people assembled in vast public squares, listened enraptured to ranting Fascist dictators ... rabble engulfed in hatred turned the world into a firestorm. That haunting memory brought with it an obligation to reacquaint the young with the meaning of mobs—the nature of human creatures raised to the boiling point by charismatic utterance.

But that Cronkite's purpose was to provide a helpful historical reminder doesn't alter his communicated meaning.

Implicit in his words of warning was an assertion that the unfamiliar groups suddenly vivid on the screen—and hitherto absent from the political stage—were markedly dissimilar to the majority, and that the decisive element in the difference wasn't social background but degree of credulousness. Unlike ordinary demonstrators, the Jacksonites embodied (in Cronkite's eyes) force reminiscent of that which, a half-century ago, escaped rational control; their behavior probably betokened incapacity to judge the motives of a Leader. Should these not ungrounded fears prove correct, the location of the group—inside or outside the "mainstream"—would be immaterial.

Here once more the perspective originates in the vision of America as a place of nearly universal membership in the imperial middle. On the mental map the dominant feature is a huge mainstream fed by tame, minuscule tributaries; moments when the tributaries burgeon and rage, flooding their borders, bespeak the onset of chaos. These untoward faces and costumes, this dearth of white men in suits, shirts and ties ... Weird sights and sounds—general indecorum— waken a sense of *foreignness*, a fear of strangers. And because the use of the masking language banishes the possibility of exploring the factor of class difference, other differences are melodramatized. These new, would-be participants can have had no share in the accumulated national experience of democratic political life, is it not so? They're unschooled in the lessons of the culture of democracy; they come upon us like a street mob. Can they truly be welcomed? "Things went awry" in Europe only yesterday. To what does this scene testify except that "things" are going awry once again, here and now?

A polity imagined to be composed of significantly different vital parts, each potent and vibrant, each conceiving its membership in the whole in unique terms, is at relative ease with the language of class—regarding it as a resource for understanding, a means of making sense of what appears at first sight strange and baffling. But the Cronkite-Sevareid polity—the media polity—believes itself to be composed uniformly of experienced civic humanists and poised middle majoritarians; it freezes when confronted with phenomena proclaiming the reality of significant difference; it cannot talk class. Denying the truth that the nature of the convention itself confirmed, refusing to trust the proven power of the culture of democracy to school *all* in its essentials and to persuade *all* of its value, the media voice of the imperial middle befuddles the nation with frights, nightmares, inapplicable history. The variegated social tableau vanishes; we're invited, ever so obliquely, to imagine hordes of swarthy malcontents—gullible aliens, unstable in crisis, pliant to any master-manipulator's hand.

Defensible Childbeaters

The most troubling masks of class are moral—those which define differences not in terms of ignorance, insensitivity, mental health, or civic illiteracy but in terms of basic moral standards. Paradox dogs such definitions, but the media are entranced with them. Quite commonly, moralistic formulations are arrived at not out of obliviousness to class but as the result of an abrupt (hence poorly thought through) dawning that class does actually warrant notice, after all, as an influence on behavior. Determined to make amends for previous neglect, inexperienced at weighing social backgrounds in their interdependencies with other forces, media minds leap to demonstrate that they've seen, they've grasped, they realize at last that a dirty little secret must be laid bare. But the zeal of the convert betrays them, and the awkwardly intense effort at redress obscures social reality instead of illuminating it.

An example: During the outcry following the beating death of Lisa Steinberg in Manhattan, an article surveying press and public reaction appeared in the Sunday think section of *The New York Times*. The writer, Mark Uhlig, quoted statistics provided by a recent Mayoral Task Force report (seven times as many fatal childbeatings occur in welfare families as in non-welfare families; ten times as many fatal childbeatings occur in black families as white families; three times as many fatal beatings occur in Hispanic families as in white families). At Uhlig's invitation, welfare officials, journalism deans and reporters covering the Steinberg case offered their views on the meaning of the outpouring of public concern.

"In this case," said Cesar A. Perales, State Commissioner of Social Services, "you're clearly dealing with a white, middle-class, professional, Jewish family that does not fit in with our notions of a family in which you'd find this kind of violence." Perales added: "I don't think we would get this kind of attention if it were a poor minority family." Norman Isaacs, a former Columbia University Journalism school dean, observed that, as journalists, "we tend to treat [child abuse] as commonplace in the black or have-not part of the community—as though this is just part of the life that goes on there." But, he continued, "I don't think that's necessarily a bias. We're operating on the best instincts we have as to what is or is not the news."

Summing up the opinions of reporters, Uhlig wrote: "Many journalists defended the intense coverage of the case by pointing out that the educational and professional background of the Steinberg family made the incident far more surprising, less defensible—and more newsworthy—than similar abuse in a desperately poor or uneducated household."

Neither Mark Uhlig nor the reporters whose views he quoted intended to widen the gap between the "desperately poor and uneducated" and others. To the contrary: they were attempting to sharpen public revulsion at Joel Steinberg's brutality, and to demonstrate their own readiness to weigh mitigating factors of deprivation that enter into criminal behavior by the poor.

But, in combination with the statistics, the statement that murderous brutality is "less defensible" among educated professionals than among the uneducated, the poor and the "minorities" falsifies the differences it purports to register. By intimating that a sliding scale based on class might appropriately replace rigid, culture-wide sanctions against cruelty, the statement implies that in some genuine respect class differences amount to moral differences. (Ambiguity erupts, as in other masking languages; "less defensible" can be read as a legalism—a reference to levels of difficulty, for defense attorneys, of different child abuse cases.) The effect is to turn attention to illusory rather than to substantive differences, thereby guaranteeing that no genuine engagement can take place between the imperial middle and those it perceives as outgroups.

On occasion the identification of social differences as moral differences is flat and unqualified. During a *Face the Nation* discussion of a 1989 Central Park gang rape and near-murder committed by juveniles, Leslie Stahl commented as follows on the accused: "But I thought they were *good* kids. Two of them were from doorman apartments ... went to parochial schools. ..."

What exactly are the substantive differences that deserve attention? The first essential for understanding them is awareness that the vast majority of the uneducated and the minorities abides by precisely the same imperatives of loving forbearance observed elsewhere in the culture. The second essential is awareness that sure knowledge of substantive class differences demands close-grained study of the comparative costs and meanings of forbearance *class by class* in the noncriminal population; it cannot be derived from statistics on outbreaks of savagery.

"What is amazing," Judge David L. Bazelon once wrote, "is that so many deprived Americans accept their lot without striking out." No offhand generalizations about intimidation or resignation can bring outsiders close to the heart of that acceptance; the task demands grounded, self-abnegating effort by the constructive imagination. When after focusing on crime rates, the voice of the imperial middle endorses as "compassionate" the thesis that defensible childbeaters exist in number among blacks and Hispanics—that the moral values of the middle are remote from those of people on the presumed margins—it confirms its own fancied superiority (we are people of discipline and sympathy), but totally conceals the nature of the differences with which it pretends to be concerned.

The power of a great newspaper to effect such concealment is obviously no mere matter of the choice of a masking vocabulary; it arises from the continuous daily translation of class differences into other terms. Measuring the cumulative moral influence exerted on behalf of the myth of classlessness, edition after edition, requires a sustained look at those processes of translation (the upcoming chapter takes such a look).

But always language holds center stage. At primitive levels the masking of class involves use of the universal language of occupational innuendo, the idioms of which disparage neutrally and offhandedly without evident arrogance or scorn. Hotel chain executives are fluent in this tongue ("a maid is a maid"), and so, too, are writers for liberal weeklies (*The Village Voice*, for instance, regularly stereotypes by vocation and ethnic given names: Hardware store salesmen "named Guido selling drill bits to muscular guys named José"). At more sophisticated levels, as we've seen, masking languages draw on the resources of science to lend authority to basic acts of dehumanization. What is striking is the national facility at generating substitutes for the language of class; it approaches the incredible and is properly thought of as the sea on which the mythology of classlessness floats.

· Chapter 7 ·

DAILY DISCOURSES

With the daily paper comes the daily myth; absent newspaper support and belief wavers. Layout, reportage, columns, and ads proclaim, on their face, the newness of the day—a break with yesterday; basic substance, on the other hand, speaks of continuity—the essential uninterruptibility of the world according to the imperial middle. What guarantees continuity is the steadiness—the reliable predictability—of the proffered explanations of social difference. Of all the functions performed by the media in service of the myth of classlessness—the invention of new heroes, new fables, new masking languages—none matches this in overall importance: the provision of daily, unvarying, simple explanations of the mystery of standing.

Simplicity is of the essence. There are but two discourses, one of superiority, the other of inferiority; the former places readers not as a social class but as persons of moral and mental distinction; the latter places outsiders not as members of a class but as people mentally and/or morally deficient. Both discourses are found at their purest in the preeminent imperial middle journal: *The New York Times*.

* * *

An example: a Sunday edition of the *Times* runs a two-thousand-word "special report" entitled: "Selling Crack/The Myth of Wealth." The front-page headline reads: DESPITE ITS PROMISE OF RICHES/THE CRACK TRADE SELDOM PAYS. The reporter, Gina Kolata, asserts at the top that "Despite the popular notion that crack sellers all drive Mercedes-Benzes, wear gold jewelry and get rich quick, most of the people in the business work round the clock, six to seven days a week, for low real wages in an atmosphere of physical threat and control." She observes further that wherever crack is sold, people speak of a "financial picture" different from the one they had hoped for, and she quotes a battery of "social scientists, ethnographers and others" describing "lives ... based on myth and self deception." A University of Colorado Medical School anthropologist who studies drug dealers declares that he goes into "their homes in the housing projects and they have nothing there." An anthropologist at John Jay College of Criminal Justice asserts that dealers "lose out financially," noting that "they don't have a Social Security number. They don't have health insurance. They don't have additional training." A San Francisco State anthropologist discloses that lookouts make only $35 for a twelve-hour shift; a sociologist at the City University of New York says he knows "lookouts in East Harlem who make only about $30 ... less than the minimum wage."

In several paragraphs the reporter details the cautionary story of a twenty-six-year-old Milwaukeean who once tried to make a living selling cocaine. A former teenage gang leader, well connected with dealers, the man sold powdered cocaine, lived constantly with a gun at his side, and found that his business was always open. ("People are coming to your house 24 hours a day—at crazy hours.") For a time he earned $600 a week, but tensions mounted. He felt "it was mandatory [to] spend money ostentatiously." He watched as "one by one his friends [in the trade] were jailed or killed," and gradually "the threat of jail and death" became unendurable. He simply gave up—quit selling cocaine and took a job "wiping cars in a car wash, for $4.50 an hour."

Other life stories recounted in the piece confirm the pattern. The experts stress that: "You'll see dealers in a big [Mercedes] Benz. But it's not theirs. Dealers exchange cars to put up a front." In her own person the reporter asserts that dealers' gold chains are often fake: "People on the streets who have bought and sold drugs and know the truth tell each other there is money to be made, that their own continuing poverty is just bad luck. They put on airs, fake courage. They bluff." The theme throughout never diverges from that announced in the headline: drug pushing is no road to success, and young people who believe "the persistent myths about opportunities" are self-deceived.

As conceived and written the story defines the situation of the young men and women involved in terms that assimilate their situations to the situations of people far better placed. Implicit is the notion that reality as experienced by incipient drug pushers consists of two sharply different, recognizably separate paths—one clear and safe, the other blocked and dangerous—between which a free choice is made. Choice *A* heads the chooser toward a solid job, steady advancement abetted by training, the security of longterm benefit packages, pension prospects, other standard perks of the middle; choice *B* offers an hour or two—or a season— of glitter, followed by jail, death, or both. Hesitating between these choices can only appear, to someone placed in the middle, close to inexplicable; choosing path *B* qualifies as stupid. The undercurrent of the story—particularly the references to faking, bluffing, and self-deception—carries a suggestion that human dimness and gullibility may bear responsibility for the drug crisis.

Different perspectives on the situation of young pushers are of course conceivable. The orderly vistas conjured up by the phrases "health insurance," "minimum wage," and "financial pictures" fail to connect with the defeat and chaos of daily street life as observed by ghetto youth. The positive sense of "training" and education assumed as normal in the piece is remote from that of people for whom school has been largely an initiation into awareness of themselves as fated losers. For inner city youth, the range of job opportunities featuring training options—jobs of the sort held out by the reporter as promising alternatives to the fake glitter of the drug trade—is rather narrower than the piece implies. And benefits packages and training programs were surely as nonexistent at the car wash to which the pusher retreated after his failure as in the drug trade itself.

But, given the fundamental purpose of such stories—to establish the basic terms of social difference in the urban setting—none of this is pertinent. The "special report" refers once in its course to the fact that "jobs for uneducated, unskilled workers [are] hard to find"; it also acknowledges that "the swagger [of the pusher] and even the small real incomes are convincing in a poverty-stricken neighborhood." But both the reporter and the trusted experts treat these points as minor. The goal of the story isn't to inquire into a community composed of people with insides of their own—people who possess mental pictures of themselves and their circumstances that are rational although at odds with the opinions of those looking down from outside. Nor is the story's function to acquaint readers with an inner landscape of despair that can clarify hidden dimensions of the "problem."

The function of the story is to fix a distance between the middle and mental darkness; once the distance is established, a preceptorial, chiding, even rebuking posture (pushers "put on airs . . . fake . . . bluff") becomes appropriate. The We-They world that emerges attributes division solely to possession or lack of intelligence (*We* see through stupid illusions/ *they* don't). One grasps that the heart of the problem is that people in urban ghettos simply aren't very bright.

This moral-mental hierarchy embodies class, not race, convictions and is fundamental to the newspaper's daily current of explanation regarding outsiders. Allusions to working people's lives are regularly accompanied by reminders that apparent class divisions are actually matters of brains. The tone varies; the point is sometimes made casually, or with tongue in cheek, sometimes by quoting without comment a working class remark presented as so glaringly ignorant or vacuous that it speaks for itself.

A *Times* television column takes up the subject of progress in the treatment of working people in sitcoms; it observes that bigoted or oafish characters (as in yesteryear's *All in the Family*) seem to be giving way to characters who are discerning and knowledgeable (*Roseanne*). Walter Goodman, the columnist, poses a question: "How did Roseanne, who doesn't travel much and is rarely caught reading anything between hard covers, get so smart, so much smarter than earlier working-class representatives [on TV] like *The Honeymooners*?" The answer:

"Why, by watching television . . . Popular [TV] shows are often imbued with the attitudes and know-how of the well-read types who write them. The shows are usually a couple

of steps ahead of the mass audience on such things as 'values.'
That's how come Roseanne, who never went to college,
proves such a shrewd psychologist of her friends' neuroses
and the antics of her kids."

In this case applauding a positive trend provides occasion
for ritual disparagement of working class intelligence. By their
own effort "working stiff types" (the columnist's phrase)
would find it hard to rise from insensitivity and bigotry; their
ascent to shrewdness about "values" is owed to helpers who,
by laboring in value-fluent Los Angeles sitcom factories, bring
light to working stiffs. Again other perspectives are conceivable. Sociological studies indicate that bigotry is more common in middle class settings than below; the most famous TV
bigot—Archie Bunker—was the invention of Norman Lear,
writer and producer, not of a manual worker; evidence isn't
available to support belief that the moral intelligence indispensable to sound rearing of children is more widespread
among the well-off than among the poor. But again none of
this is pertinent. The discourse is about the deficiencies of
those outside the imperial middle; it has no obligation to
undermine itself.

Education pages are especially rich in the explanatory
mode. An "About Education" column headed TWO WHO SCOUR
THE COUNTRYSIDE FOR "DIAMONDS IN THE ROUGH" reports on an
admissions officer and a biology professor employed at Mid-
dlebury College in Vermont. The pair visit remote sections
of the country—"Wisdom High School in St. Agatha, Me.,
Hope High School in North Dakota, and Bullfrog Junction,
Me."—in search of students "to counterbalance the kids from
prep schools or suburban high schools." The columnist, Fred
Hechinger, is on the side of these recruiters, sharing their
hope of finding "some 'superkids,' who [get] no guidance in

school and no support at home," and "rescu[ing] them from rural isolation and poverty by showing them the way to college." The clear assumption is that raw talent can be found in the hinterland and trained up to eligibility for the elites.

But the story's emphasis falls less on raw talent than on the theme that those coming up from the bottom—from "rural isolation" and "no support at home"—are fugitives from extreme benightedness. Life in the hinterland is bare of challenge, satisfaction, or delight; college is a world uniformly elevating and stimulating. Noting that many of the "rough diamonds" have "parents who are not high school graduates," the columnist offers a sampling of responses to the Middle-bury scouts: "My dad is a fisherman, and he can do a lot of things," said a student facing rescue. "Why go to college?" "What do you mean about applying?" asked another. Callowness on this order (says the no-comment style of quotation) bears no comment. Yet again an alternative perspective is imaginable. Decently founded feelings of respect for an elder could claim admiration; so might recognition that true self-sufficiency may lie in real-life competencies as opposed to credit lines and lists of emergency phone numbers.

But again those perspectives are irrelevant. The function of the story is to serve the imperial middle understanding that college (preferably a "good" college) holds the key to cultivation and intellectuality and that rural isolation means dark night for the mind. It's not to the point that jobs demanding natural observation, navigational skills, and the ability to bring an ailing motor back to life under lowering skies are perhaps better categorized by class than by demand upon intelligence. The function of the discourse is to place those "below" as people of ignorance, not as people belonging to a class: not as people adapting to *their* social reality as presumed betters adapt to theirs, not as people whose mental worlds are stored differently but are nevertheless stored, not as people some of whom may well achieve freedom from servility denied to their betters.

So disciplined is the newspaper's discourse on the social ladder as, in reality, an intelligence/character ladder that a dispatch will venture to assert—in a manner suggesting that dispute is out of the question—that concern about children's safety or schooling is restricted to the affluent. A story date-lined Chicago describes as follows a conflict emerging as "young middle-class families move into redeveloped inner-city neighborhoods":

> After developers transformed a lifeless, abandoned in-dustrial district into an upscale neighborhood on the city's near South Side, the young professionals who moved in—mostly white, but with a substantial black minority—asked the Board of Education to build a school for their children. South Loop Elementary was completed last year, just a stone's throw from the new condominiums in Dearborn Park.
>
> But the school is also just a short walk from Hilliard Homes, a public housing project plagued by drug traffic and other crime problems. A bitter struggle ensued over which children would be allowed to attend it. *The conflict pits the issue of fairness for the poorer children against the desire of the affluent parents to send their children to a good, safe school.*

The sentence I italicize spells out the basic assumption: if the poor battle for their children's right to be admitted to a good school, they're moved by an obsession with "fairness," not by a desire similar to that of the affluent.

No single example or set of examples, though, can give much inkling of the immense utility of the style of discourse under examination; its power flows from recurrence—from the firm, steady, almost undeviating adherence, day by day, to the concept of moral/intellectual difference as unimpeachable social indicator. Under the force of exceptional circumstances—witness the Steinberg case—the paper's certainty can be momentarily shaken. But those moments pass and certainty returns. When referring to Them (i. e., when engaged in the discourse of inferiority), the paper is steadfastly loyal to the model of explanation that rules out class as an influence, and holds the factors of intelligence and moral fiber to be decisive.

The discourse of superiority is a shade more complicated, owing to the need ceaselessly to translate affluence into other terms. Signals are passed from day to day that the ideal reader of *The New York Times* is a person whose financial identity isn't determined by hourly wage rates. Securities markets are extensively covered and advice is regularly offered on such topics as how to secure respect at one's investment house. (MAKING NICE TO YOUR BROKER, runs a comradely head over a recent four-column piece on this subject.)

But financial identity is thought of as marginal to true distinction—an adjunct of more significant primary qualities, among which intelligence and taste are pivotal. The flood of foreign news on the inside pages of the newspaper's front section defines the audience as inquiring, non-provincial, and possessed of the funds of background information necessary to order and interpret the material. And knowledgeableness in this sector is presented as simply one aspect of the general versed-ness that's the actual foundation of distinction.

The discourse of superiority is unrelenting, therefore, in its pursuit of questions of taste and quality. The Home section may carry a dozen pieces that imply a reader of considerable discretionary spending power—pieces about replicas of eighteenth-century desks by master carvers, about the situation of a foxhunter who switches "from horses to square-headed [croquet] mallets from Lillywhites of London" following a hip injury in a point-to-point race, or about a complex redecoration of a multi-room co-op with views of the Central Park reservoir and Fifth Avenue skyline. The mallets are dear, the desks cost $20,000 per replica, the apartment close to a million.

But the prices remain incidental. Fashion shows ("For some parties, a ball gown is de rigueur"), like investment counsel (MAKING NICE TO YOUR BROKER) define their true audience as the community of the bright: those who can spot a gaffe at a glance and are first of all relishers of urban knowhow in every sector of life. Size of income is immaterial in this discourse; quickness is closer to the core.

As is self-madeness. The discourse of superiority excludes layabouts, the beholden, and the irresolute. Its assumed participants aren't merely persons of intelligence and taste; they're resourceful, take-charge persons who earned their place the old-fashioned way. The central themes of the mythology of classlessness—mobility, individual responsibility, choice—resound everywhere in the newspaper, now in formal editorials or casual pieces by staff members, now in advice to non-elites that turns up, boxed but without comment, in the news pages.

A network television program on "Black in White America" hints that blacks living in the projects can't be held wholly responsible for their individual fates. A self-identified

DAILY DISCOURSES ■

African-American *Times* staffer—Don Wycliff—answers in "The Editorial Notebook," calling the hint "strange illogic or fatuousness," proposing that blacks must face up to the truth that nobody can change their situation except themselves, and offering as an inspiring example "Charles Alfred (Chief) Anderson, who trained the Tuskegee Airmen, the nation's first black fighter pilots, during World War II. . . . 'I've seen a time when I couldn't even get a ride in an airplane,' the Chief said. 'And I've been chased off airport fields. And, of course, what I had to do, I had to go and buy an airplane, say, "Hell, I'm going to learn anyhow.' "

Or the *Times* editorializes impatiently at people who whine about conspicuous consumption—prigs who denounce birthday party extravaganzas mounted by one or another tycoon. "Why so much moralizing criticism?" it asks, and suggests that the critics are "expressing something deeper than reasons, something unlikely to be responsive to debate"—probably envy. It then moves on to the classic imperial middle theme: "Even moralists may acknowledge that there's a silver lining in modern plutocratic parties. Kings once invited lords to their extravaganzas. Now the principle is not nobility but mobility. Malcolm Forbes did not invite Henry Kissinger, child of Fuerth, Germany, or Walter Cronkite, child of St. Joseph, Mo., because of their lineage. The Parties of August may have glittered tastelessly, but at least in terms of personal achievement, they were open to the public."

The position is roughly the same when the newspaper responds to a perceived threat to the future of faith in individual responsibility. It reminds its audience of who they are and of how their excellence has been constituted by printing, as "Washington Talk" (at some remove from the editorial and letters columns, and the Op-Ed page), excerpts from an article in *The Public Interest* by Isabel V. Sawhill spelling out what is meant by responsibility:

> Laws and mores may vary with time and place, but in America today certain norms are widely held. First, children are expected to study hard and complete at least high school. Second, young people are expected to refrain from conceiving children until they have the personal and financial resources to support them; this usually means delaying childbearing until they have completed school and can draw on a regular salary. Third, adults are expected to work at a steady job, unless they are retired, disabled or ... supported by their spouse. Fourth, everyone is expected to obey the laws.
>
> These are social obligations. Those who fulfill them are unlikely to be chronically poor. If they are poor despite having abided by the rules, society is much more likely to come to their rescue. This is and (with the possible exception of the 1960's) always has been the nature of the social contract. The problem is too many people who are not fulfilling their end of the bargain; these people constitute the underclass. Have such people failed society, or has society failed them?

These thoughts appear under the slug: "Exact Words."

"Short of genius," as Péguy once wrote, "a rich man cannot imagine poverty."

Yet more important than intelligence, taste, and self-madeness in shaping the discourse of superiority is the sense of noblesse oblige. The *Times* defines its reader as someone who wishes full information on public and private research documenting hardships common in the bottom tiers of the American population ... as someone who welcomes and editorially endorses innovative legislative proposals designed to ease those hardships ... as someone impressed by an institution that sustains a major urban charity (the "Neediest Cases") for decades.

The newspaper's solidarity with affluence, in short, means something other than what it might appear to mean at first glance—or than what might be deduced from the profusion in advertising of expensive goods and services, or from the concentration, in features, on luxo restaurants, neighborhoods, hobbies. Affluence is understood as but a symptom of superiority that's actually traceable to solider qualities: intelligence, taste, public spirit, responsibility, readiness to rule. The *Times* conceives itself as spokesperson for a readership awash in these qualities. And it is this solidarity that closes the newspaper's social world, rendering editor and ideal reader alike indifferent to the concepts of distance and self-criticism, and driving both in the direction of colonialist auto-didacticism.

But that is another subject. What's at stake here is the character of the newspaper's support of the mythology of classlessness—the support, to repeat, of explanation. The standing of outsiders, working people, and bottom dogs is explained daily as the result of weak minds and shaky morals. Readers are equally well informed as to the causes of their own membership in the imperial middle. And together in the package with these explanations comes steady assurance that other perspectives are needless. When one knows about oneself that one is generous, prepared to push for every bottom dog who takes one's word about what's right ... when one knows, further, that one cares about higher education, the arts, all that ... when one knows what it is to sweat a little to make something of oneself in plain pecuniary terms ... when all these conditions obtain, it cannot be rational to burden oneself with the obligation of behaving as though perspectives different from one's own warrant earnest regard. Little exists in the world of fishermen and working stiff types upon which approval could be seriously bestowed.

The arts of exorcism and erasure practiced in the media shape, in sum, four versions of class: as a fantasy from which the sensible and rightminded awake in good time; as a dressup game enabling us to "get out of ourselves"—turn omni, meet new people, have fun; as an unreliable, excessively subjective indicator which, thanks to Science and Progress, need no longer be consulted; as a veil shrouding the real—i.e., moral/ intellectual—differences in our midst.

Dispute about the sociopsychological effect of these erasures is inevitable. Those who profit, commercially or otherwise, from the continuing vitality of the myth of classlessness will represent the effect as positive. The transformation of class differences into a fantasy, game, or archaism reflects repugnance at a society structured along clear class lines; the repugnance proves the survival, in this country, of faith in classless solidarity as a value; whether or not the value is founded on actualities, the media in promoting it help us remain open to each other.

The opposed view—my own—has already been stated; it is that the effect is harmful. Transforming class differences into differences of other kinds, or into material for games and fantasies, strips us of knowledge both about each other and about the forces and processes that figure in the shaping of human identity. Neither the omni- nor the renunciation-sensibility is cruel, and, arguably, the same can be said of those who deploy technical and moral languages in characterizing the socially distant as mentally or morally ill, or as culturally or intellectually deficient. But the edifice of opinion thus constructed has prejudice for its substructure and is clearly underfurnished with fact. Inside its walls we live with no grasp of the substance or meaning of the differences among us.

Resolving the dispute about the effect of class erasures, however, won't bring us closer to the goals of understanding set at the start of this work. Media influence is enormous and deserves the extended attention paid it here; the motive of those who discount the influence is usually that of offsetting criticism; were this giant opinion and fable-fabricating industry to transform its present assumptions about class, the country would quickly feel the difference. But it's undeniable that much of the influence is in the nature of confirmation. The purveyed versions of class are acceptable not because of the CBS/White House/*New York Times* aegis but because nothing in them triggers outraged resistance.

And this isn't the mere result of passivity or the sense of powerlessness; the true explanations lie deep in the American psyche and American history. The casual assumptions outlined in the early chapters of this work, belief in "equality," in the absence of "levels," in the fundamental openness of the society, in nearly universal membership in the imperial middle—all of this has experiential foundations. Comprehending the American sense of class as reflected in the media and in real-life behavior requires that these foundations, too, be laid bare.

· *Part III* ·
ROOTS

·

Chapter 8

SCHOOL: THE FAIRNESS ZONE

*A*class that conceives of it-self as all-encompassing is hardly an unprecedented phenom-enon in the social history of the West. Marx and Engels claimed that each new class is compelled, as it develops, "to represent its interests as the common interests of all the members of society," and to represent its ideas "as the only rational, universally valid ones." In our time the means by which the interests of the relatively powerful (and allegedly classless) can be represented as universal are more various than before. And protest on behalf of the relatively powerless, whose interests are treated as non-existent, has lost vitality.

Yesterday's language of resistance dared to accuse and chastise—spoke of crimes, victimization, dark satanic mills —evoked idealized peasants abused by a heartless nobility and (later) independent yeomen and artisans who were happy and self-respecting until ruined by the labor-exploiting, skills-destroying system called capitalism. Popular uprisings testified to the might of the images; even though swiftly (often brutally) crushed, the protests warned of an oppositional fury seemingly beyond cooling.

It cooled. On American shores bourgeois means middle not hateful nowadays; utopian visions of individualistic, self-realizing small farmers and craftsmen (as distinguished from dehumanized operatives in plants and office buildings) stir nobody's imagination. Pastoral taste is catered for in hobby, garden, and wilderness stores, and the term *proletariat* has a comic valence. Among the coolants were many forces cited by pundits in explaining why our political scene lacks a socialist or labor party: the feeling in the American working class for the sanctity of property (both Tocqueville and Engels were struck by that); the abundance of consumer goods; the spirit of egalitarianism; a past not indelibly marked by bitter struggles for political and economic rights (with large exceptions: blacks and women); unique geographic and demographic circumstances; and (once more) mobility.

The historical interaction of these impersonal forces will be probed shortly. But the present and near-present—personal experience, memory, self-concepts—are crucial to the psychology of classlessness; in them lie the ultimate origins of the omni sensibility and the determination to shrug off every apparent hierarchy and ban the language of class. The will to believe the mythology of classlessness is rooted in personal narrative: the stories of our self-mythologizing lives. *Once upon a time*, says the voice of memory, *I lived through a situation in which rank order was based on ability, work held the key to privilege, all possessed the right to earn privilege, and the allocation of rewards was disinterested and just. I and the others stood equal at the starting line in this situation, dependent solely on personal resources. I was free to race with the pacemakers or hang back and finish last. I knew the contest was consequential for life fortunes. I knew that doing better or worse was up to me.*

I knew that in this situation—the place and time wherein I individually determined my fate and fashioned my unique self—fairness ruled.

For the American majority the name of the original situation in question is, of course, school. According to an accumulating body of opinion research, the unlucky and badly paid who protest in interviews at their lot often volunteer that they did have a chance—school—and blew it through fault of their own. Successful and well-off interviewees, for their part, accompany expressions of sympathy with the unfortunate with volunteered assertions that the competition in which they gained their own high place was in no way fixed. If, as a millionaire President in the White House put it, Life is unfair, school wasn't. *I earned my edge, shaped my future, under the rule of fairness; the race that settled things was the same length for all.*

A number of familiar assumptions about intelligence, the profession of teaching, and public policy concerning the structure and financing of education enter into the sense of school as a fairness zone. One assumption is that intellectual ability—quickness, schoolsmarts, a good mind, college material—is an essence that an individual possesses as the result of biogenetic causes, and develops or fails to develop as a matter of personal volition. Another is that ability can surface anywhere at any time and is quickly recognizable by teachers and testing agencies expert at detecting it. Another is that schools and teachers deal exclusively with ability in its purity, not with extraneous items such as pupils' background, appearance, clothes, economic status. Still another is that school is alert to sudden awakenings and late bloomings. (The authorities see to it that transfer is feasible from vocational to academic tracks and from two-year to four-year institutions of higher learning; private sector, profit-making schools are licensed to serve those whose career decisions —from computer programming to cooking—don't fit orthodox academic calendars or curricula; qualified candidates are allowed to begin professional education in mid-life, etc.)

And in addition there's the assumption that policy regarding appropriations for the educational process reflects a more than casual interest, on the part of the public, in preventing domination by unearned privilege. (The interest manifests itself in scholarship and loan funds, state subsidies, efforts to equalize expenditure per pupil among school districts, other economic initiatives.)

Understandings of these concepts differ from sector to sector of the population. In upscale quarters pure ability connotes "giftedness" and is admired. Elsewhere it can connote clever facility in a minority member learning to con white folks, and may be patronized as gutless. Among people who don't work with their hands, belief in intellectual ability as a distinct, separable, biopsychic essence is accompanied by certainty that differences in occupation spring from differences in smartness and giftedness (the best minds head for the professions, slow people learn trades). People who work with their hands don't invariably share—sometimes resent—this view.

Even the principle that public policy seeks to modify unearned privilege means different things to different people. In 1988 Princeton, New Jersey spent $7,015 per public school pupil; in the same year Camden, New Jersey spent $4,500 per pupil; only 7 percent of Princeton pupils failed standard proficiency tests, whereas a percentage eleven times greater failed in Camden. Establishment liberals (including a sitting judge) read the statistics and related material as grounds for overhauling the state's school financing system in order to assure educational equity. More than a few Princeton parents, on the other hand, opposed to sending their children away, read the same numbers in the context of public school versus private school; fairness, in their view, is what individual communities achieve by taxing themselves heavily enough to create mini-Choates within walking distance. And in many working class communities talk of equalizing pupil expenditures or transforming a local high school into Choate can seem airy. Concern about quality is likely to center, as in Yonkers in 1988, on fear of invasion by a minority perceived as threatening to the safety and values of the majority, or, within the minority, on fear of exclusion and persecution.

Pausing over such differences is a useful way of guarding against excessive homogenization of attitudes toward school. Different sectors of society have different agendas, hence define equity in different terms; the price of ignoring the differences is a return to imperial middle universalism.

But the fact of differences isn't in this instance the central fact: what matters more is the exceptional breadth of agreement on fairness and evenhandedness as school norms. Certainty that career prospects are related to school performance cuts across social classes from old money to new money through the poverty line; so, too, does trust in the impartially grading teacher, and assurance of the weight of personal choice. The need for vigilance is acknowledged ("Keep politics out of the school"). But the educational process overall is seen as both clean and potent, capable of creating a degree of equality through its own impartiality, capable also of guaranteeing all children—regardless of their parents' success or failure in life—some chance of self-propelled upward movement. The consensus supports the conviction that school is an institution crucial to the survival of an opportunity society. And not uncommonly, as youthful experience is idealized over the years, school becomes memory's democratic home base. Equality on the starting line is recalled as the original reality that later experience—mere illusion, mere pretense —sadly obscures. Hence the popularity of the class reunion (thousands occur yearly). For an hour that institution refreshes memory of the levelness of the first playing field, sanctioning denials of class, affirming the rough justice of life.

All democratic societies tend to view education positively, and special circumstances in this society intensify the tendency. In opting for racial and ethnic variety, America chose to add citizens by the tens of millions whose presumed dreams of Americanization could be realized only through schooling. And the succeeding dream of preserving ethnic traditions was also set under school custodianship. It doesn't follow, though, that school's rise to autonomy and consecration was inevitable. Autonomy was hard-gained, with paradox and accident playing roles in its achievement.

Two developments were decisive, says hindsight. The first allayed suspicion that school was cowed by the rich, therefore bound to be biased. The second lifted school (in popular estimate) above conflicting interests, beyond coercion by influences other than that of objective truth.

Neither development came swiftly. The common schooling system in place in America by the mid-nineteenth century drew together youngsters of widely varying background in a single course of study; the system's founders regarded inclusiveness as a national imperative. But those same founders were far from conceiving of the system as an equalizer. Early readers and grammars took class for granted, preaching resignation, not ambition. McGuffey Readers, in fables entitled "The Rich Boy" and "The Poor Boy," recommended that rich pupils treat poor ones kindly, and that poor pupils accept their condition. "If I were a man," Rich Boy declares, "and had plenty of money, I think no person who lived near me should be very poor." "I have often been told," Poor Boy remarks, "that it is God who makes some poor and others rich; that the rich have many troubles which we know nothing of; and that the poor, if they are but good, may be very happy: indeed, I think that when I am good, nobody can be happier than I am."

With the invention of the high school, moreover, "common" in common schooling underwent redefinition. Extended academic education was available to all, but in practice was provided only to pupils who could afford to stay out of the labor market long enough to receive it. (U.S. Office of Education statistics show that in 1890 there were almost seven times as many teenagers at work as at school.) And it was broadly acknowledged that pupils in the immensely larger, bottom tier of the two-tier educational system were being prepared for factory work. Authorities responded to corporate complaint about unruly workers by insisting that they themselves understood their obligation to produce disciplined plant hands. One school superintendent and U.S. educational commissioner asserted in 1871 that it was because factory life requires "conformity to the time of the train, to the starting of work in the manufactory," that "the first requisite of the school is *Order.*" And he added: "The pupil must have his lessons ready at the appointed time, must rise at the tap of the bell, move to the line, return; in short, go through all the evolutions with equal precision."

During the first decades of common schooling, in short,

the voice of the system wasn't easily distinguished from voices of moneyed interests. School admitted all comers, taught all comers literacy and numeracy, showed all comers how to live peaceably with each other. (Offensive to our ears, the Rich Boy–Poor Boy fables themselves represented, in their period, evenhanded openness of a sort.) But even as they were included, working people were fixed in their place, offered little that would inspire loyalty, gratitude, or belief in the fairness of things.

Change came partly because of a developing struggle for control of schools. Periodically, industry leaders sought to displace school administrators, abolish unitary common schooling, and institute job-skills training. Labor reaction was mixed; from the early workingmen's trade associations and parties (the 1820s and 1830s) straight through to the formation of the major, end-of-the-century unions, workers at moments saw advantage in separate, strictly vocational education, and sometimes opposed it only out of an instinct for job protection. (Business-run job-training institutes were on occasion seen as schemes for producing strikebreakers.)

Gradually, though, larger issues—those meant to be captured in the phrase educational equity—commenced surfacing. Grasping that business-run schools were inimical to their own interests, educators encouraged labor to stand firm for common schooling—to believe that it offered children of the working class a chance at full democratic citizenship and self-betterment that the alternative denied. As responsiveness to this theme deepened, administrators rejected plant-hand preparation and, in official rhetoric, widened the moral mission of school. Chicago's first woman superintendent of schools, Ella Flagg Young, declared in 1909 that she did not believe "in training the young to belong to a lower industrial class." An unfamiliar idea was ripening: school as an activist in the crusade for social justice.

Economic circumstance speeded the growth of trust between working class parents and teachers. Poorly paid, disenfranchised (because female), most teachers in the early decades of this century had reason to identify with working class constituencies. (Unionization prolonged the sympathy, even though subsequent generations of teachers would increasingly label themselves middle class.) The coming of truly bad times—the Depression, mass unemployment—strengthened labor's commitment to the school as one of the few institutions which, if not precisely on workingpeople's side, at least didn't stand to make money by wringing workers and their families.

The emerging solidarity of the community of educators and the ranks of labor, each holding school out to the other as a locus of hope, might in time have entangled education in new conflict, rendering idealization impossible. Among the well-off, after all, favorable attitudes toward school stemmed less from appreciation of a democratizing force capable of raising the low and leveling the high than from enthusiasm for the secondary school system as a class preserve. And losing the fight for control had hardly reduced businessmen's suspicion of public education. The most effective weapon educators deployed in the late nineteenth and early twentieth century campaign for autonomy was the concept of school as the adjunct of upward mobility. But that deployment opened up lines of dispute demanding—hindsight speaks again—new weapons.

One emerged: science. The public consequences of the triumph of social science in our time lie beyond quick reckoning; one major consequence was the extrication of school from social conflict and the laying of a foundation for the claim that education advanced the cause of justice concretely and objectively. Mass "scientific" intelligence testing during World War I intrigued the nation. Graduate schools of education and school administrators stepped forward as guardians and representatives of a precious methodology capable of functioning as the right arm of equity, freeing evaluation and management of human potential from age-old favoritism and prejudice. In the first half of this century science worship was everywhere, permeating all areas of American life—business, politics, religion, art. But it was in the field of education that the enthusiasm most dramatically connected itself with the ideal of democratic equity. A revolution fought partly in the hope of banishing arbitrary inequality had been followed by a century in which the specter of inequality had returned; the new sciences of psychology and administration promised to ground fairness in impersonal standards; through Stanford-Binet true merit would rise to the top and the original American promise would be realized. And schoolpeople alone—*professionals*—were competent to put the tool to use.

The rise or fall in public esteem of any institution touching the lives of an entire population is, needless to say, a complex phenomenon. Definitive word can't be spoken about which force—the original commitment to inclusiveness, the defeat of business and industry school takeover bids, the upsurge of science as the handmaid of equity—most directly furthered the process of idealization. What is clear is that, over a period of a century, different social and intellectual sectors came to have strong reason for doubting that school ever would or could sell them out. From here the step was short to belief in school the equalizer.

* * *

It is, regrettably, a mistaken belief. During the past three to four decades many educational researchers and historians have worked at the task of explaining why—and at measuring the distance between a meritocratic school system and the system as it is. The pioneering contribution was a mid-century study of the class dimensions of the treatment of poor, middle, and upper middle class pupils by teachers and principals in one midwestern high school. The most influential research —that of the Coleman Commission—was conducted for the U.S. Congress, at the height of the civil rights movement. Inquiry since then has ranged freely over the school and college spectrum, from educational expenditures in relation to pupil performance, to early scholastic ability in relation to ultimate college attendance, to curriculum as abettor of class segmentation.

The Coleman Report (1966) established that class identity determined student achievement from start to finish— because it shaped attitudes toward teachers, familiarity with the materials of learning, preparatory experiences of language and reason-giving, and the environment of study. (The most recent confirmation and updating of Coleman appeared, in 1987, in William Julius Wilson's *The Truly Disadvantaged: The Inner City, the Underclass and Public Policy*; Wilson's evidence showed that quality of student performance continues to be unrelated to per-pupil expenditure and other non-class variables.)

Other research has shown that well-off students with weak academic records are far more likely to attend college than poor students with strong records; that multi-track, open transfer systems create class enclaves not fluidity; that arrangements in state-supported higher education function similarly (low subsidies for the least advantaged attending two-year colleges, high subsidies for the most advantaged attending flagship universities); and that scholarship funds advertised as democratizing influences in private colleges and universities are frequently awarded to students with family incomes of $100,000 and more per year.

A large body of inquiry has suggested, moreover, that public school teachers' conceptions of "ideal" pupils typically fuse responses to class-connected accent, appearance, manner, and deportment with responses to "natural or inborn intelligence"; similar class skewing is noted in testing agencies. The verbal behavior of middle and upper middle children, identified as "intelligent," becomes a standard of evaluation.

Often in the past quarter-century writers and commentators aware of these and related studies have gone so far as to indict public education and standardized testing, charging that both qualify as conscious conspiracies against factory and office workers, tradespeople, "unskilled" laborers. Schools are presented as socioculturally biased institutions whose primary function is to assure that top occupations aren't glutted with credentialed candidates, while preventing the spread of doubt and cynicism about the system as a whole. One thrust of the attacks is directed at curriculum and teaching methods, which are seen as systematically disparaging the knowledge and values of the largest sector of the population—the working class.

According to this argument, school everywhere takes middle and upper middle class understandings of experience as its standard. It allows post-school status systems—such as that which places mechanics below engineers—to infect the classroom. It refuses to teach scientific principles and theory in shop classes. It gives small motor repair no place in introductory physics. It automatically awards an edge, in arts and humanities education, to those at ease, because of home experience, with the materials that middle and upper middle class opinion traditionally holds worthy of "analysis," "appreciation," "discussion." It denies intellectual attention to disciplined excellence in the activities—skills, crafts, practical arts, sports—with which the majority is most conversant and comfortable. And, through the artifices of professionalization, it excludes millions of knowers and workers from the experience of knowledge-sharing, to no social end except that of subordination.

Philosophers of education, economists, and socialist revolutionaries are among those who, in the recent past, have levied these or similar charges. Rebuttals stress, among other points, that international studies indicate structural rigidity in education is less marked here than abroad, and that, in America, neither vocational nor non-vocational education has ever been geared solely to occupational demands; school invariably provides competencies beyond those required by employers. A better complaint would be that the left critique, like conventional sociological research, has failed to reach a general audience. In consequence both the extent and nature of class influence on school go unnoticed, as does the role of illusion in sustaining faith in school the equalizer.

For a time in the Eighties anxiety about education seemed on the verge of shaking that faith. The decade began with a pessimistic Department of Education study, *A Nation at Risk*, and ended with a declaration by the incoming President that education deserved to be among the highest priorities of the Chief Executive: "I want to become the Education President." But although increased public concern about "poor learning atmospheres" in urban systems has transformed education into a "problem area," it hasn't effectively challenged school's iconographic status.

One reason for this is the iron consistency with which educational discourse marginalizes unfairness—focuses chiefly on failure to deliver reading and writing skills to racial and ethnic minorities. The point is made that blacks and Hispanics are "disadvantaged," and that possibly 10 percent of the nation's schools—those dealing with inner city children—are so poorly equipped, staffed, and managed that they're incapable of providing fair opportunity to their student bodies. Political candidates and editorial writers warn that school authorities have failed to arouse, in city and state governments, a proper sense of their public duty to provide special help. But the framing of the issue conceals that the troubles of inner city schools are a special, highly publicized symptom of conditions of inequity that extend far beyond ghettos and barrios. Dropouts and "greasers" who aren't black or Hispanic vastly outnumber the entire American school population of minority students. They're the children of parents whose own experiences of academic English, History, Foreign Language, and Science were frustrating—conducive mainly to doubt that book learning is connected with the realities of practical life and work.

And these parents, to repeat, truly are the majority. It's in the working class at large, not alone in the ghetto (wrongly conceived as separable from the working class), that poetry speaks more often as sport than as Edgar Allan Poe, and that independent study and recreation concentrate on speed shops and soaps instead of upon piano lessons or the elders' favorite novels by Jane Austen.

But the notion that only for minorities is school an alien culture neatly excises both the fairness problem and the education problem from the broader realities of a class society. Four, five, and six decades ago, educational commentary and criticism didn't blink at those realities. A 1922 book on *The Selective Character of American Secondary Education* states flatly that: "The public high school is attended quite largely by the children of the more well-to-do classes. This affords us the spectacle of a privilege being extended at public expense to those very classes that already occupy the privileged positions in modern society. The poor are contributing to provide secondary education for the children of the rich, but are either too poor or too ignorant to avail themselves of the opportunities which they help to provide." Twenty years later an academic study based on classroom observation noted that: "Most lower-class children do not understand or appreciate the teacher's efforts. In turn, the teacher tends to neglect the lower-class children if she does not actually discriminate against them. They do not reward her with obedience and affection, and she does not reward them with affection, good marks, and special approval. Conversely, when the teacher finds a lower-class child who does respond to her efforts, who does seem to understand middle-class standards, she is the more interested and puts in extra effort where she thinks she can do some good."

But more recently protocol demands a near-total excision of class—hedging and equivocation about every mode of inequity that can't be "minoritized." Signs of the excision abound in newspaper stories and popular culture, as well as in academic analyses. Debate about "remediation" isolates minority schools; diagnosis treats internal influences—lazy, permissive, badly educated teachers and principals—as responsible for school failures.

Item: the principal of a largely black, Paterson, New Jersey, school patrols the corridors with megaphone and base-ball bat, locks firedoors (against undesirable intruders), expels indolent students, and succeeds in restoring order to a failed school. Fired by his school board, he's hailed as a pathfinder by the White House and provided with a position in the Department of Education by the sitting Secretary. *Black kids deserve a chance to learn and Joe Clark gave it to them.*

Item: a fiction film called *Stand and Deliver* (1988), based on the experience of a real-life Los Angeles high school teacher, tells how the man manages to teach calculus to a class of initially uninterested, unmotivated minority students. (The actual teacher, Jaime Escalante, was named a hero during the 1988 presidential debates.) Tough, streetsmart, knowl-edgeable not only about math but about the unrealized abil-ities of his students, the teacher is also resourceful in circumventing obstacles set in his path by school adminis-trators. He coaches, cajoles, browbeats, inspires, works long after school and on weekends, and produces a class of calculus stars. At one point there's a conflict between the teacher and the Educational Testing Service, which suspects him and his class of cheating. But teacher and tester alike share a devotion to fairness, and in the end that value prevails.

Item: E. D. Hirsch, a respected English professor, argues in a bestseller—*Cultural Illiteracy* (1987)—that the edu-cation problem amounts simply to a matter of cultural illit-eracy among the minorities. "Disadvantaged children" lack the background knowledge necessary for comprehension of most assigned texts, says Hirsch, but if teachers set them to work learning definitions of key terms (5,000 in number, ranging from *andante* to *sociobiology*), they'll overcome the deficiencies. "If we begin an acculturative program in early grades—that is, if we systematically provide the needed background information from the earliest possible age through third grade—then," says Hirsch, "we can overcome a lot of the knowledge deficit of disadvantaged children.... In my view, the most significant educational reform we could undertake would be to put all children on a level playing-field in literacy skills by the beginning of fourth grade."

Fairness once more. And again the conjunction of two leading ideas: inequity as the exception (a minority distress), fairness as the pedagogical obsession. At times the continuing popular and academic trust in school as the equalizer seems actually dependent on the "urban school crisis." The overt function of the crisis is to draw to a head doubt about the health of the democratic ideal of educational equity. The latent function is to lance the doubt by enabling political and educational authority to demonstrate that even tiny infractions of the rule of fairness (there can be no others) rouse fierce democratic concern.

But dramas of "concern" at most refurbish belief; they could never father it. In the mythology of school-and-life fairness the concerned educator plays a cameo part; the only true indispensables are the racers, the starting line, and the potent personal will. And it bears emphasizing that the story of the race seems as seductive to the defeated as to the victors. Again excessive homogenization looms as a danger. Scarsdale High School juniors prepping for an English Advanced Placement test are alert to a national context—a horizon of opportunity—different from that, say, of youngsters of the same age completing an apprentice training program in a predominantly Polish high school in northwest Detroit. There are numberless contests; a union apprenticeship in a well-paid trade carries a life-promise different from that implicit in an acceptance letter from the director of admissions at Yale. But in all races there are losers, and at all levels talk of the race is permeated by themes of personal choice and individual responsibility, and by comparisons of "pure" ability and talent.

When youngsters aware of their difficulties with schoolwork compare themselves with successful students, they speak not of teachers or of life-circumstances, only of "intelligence." (Recall the Chicago schoolboy who when asked by an authority figure why other pupils, who aren't hustling newspapers with him at 6 A.M., do better than he, responded: "They're smarter.") Grownups looking back at a lifetime of unrewarding, poorly paid labor see poor choices of their own as the cause—acts of individual bad judgment. *I should never have quit school* is a refrain in the extended interviews with members of the working class quoted in Robert Lane's pioneering *Political Ideology* [1962]; some responsibility is assigned to parents who didn't insist on school attendance, but in the main the speakers blame themselves.

And, predictably, winners praise themselves. Elite liberal arts college student bodies are composed largely of high-achieving children with family incomes in the top tenth percentile. Well brought up, seldom pompous, they adopt tones of sadness and frustration when discussing—in interviews—the gap that widened between themselves and non-achievers. Two separating factors are mentioned. The first is the choice, by the non-achievers, of idleness. Inexplicably, disastrously, the non-achievers simply would not *work*, preferring to hang out at malls. By this act "they threw away their future."

The second factor cited is venturesomeness. During years of academic committee service, the present writer has read a fair number of "autobiographical statements" composed by Rhodes, Marshall, Truman, and other fellowship candidates introducing themselves to jurors. Almost by convention the achievers point to entries in their record attesting their readiness to "try everything" in the line of learning experiences. In the highly developed American lesson culture of the Eighties, these experiences include a variety of privately contracted-for instruction—dressage, the bassoon, wilderness survival technique, ballet, dance skating, tennis, chess, Russian, more. "There was only one rule in my family: you had to try everything. You had to give it a fair try and afterward, if you didn't like it, okay: Quit. But you had to make the effort."

The sentence-sounds carry the inner concept of self: independent, open to possibility, aware of the endless range of pleasures and satisfactions life offers to those eager to seize the grape, unafraid of embarrassment or failure, delighting in new experiences, proud of the capacity for commitment. Habitually, that capacity is seen as a personal trait; habitually, expensive advantages and options are understood to be, at bottom, self-made.

The determination to see them thus underscores the interdependency of the themes of classlessness and unconditionedness in the American psyche. A non-sectarian shrine of the will, as well as of egalitarian moral idealism, school feeds dreams of personal potency, fantasies of self-creation. I am myself alone. What you see is what you get. The need to claim unconditionedness breathes throughout whole lifetimes; school's significance is lessened not a whit by the admission that no single institution or gesture or array of memories can meet the need once for all. As representative citizens, self-mythologizing, individualistic choosers-of-our-separate-paths, we re-invent the school story—the starting line, the momentous decision, the personal turning point—time after time, insistently, lovingly, Frost in one ear, Sinatra in the other. (*Two roads diverged in a wood. I did it my way.*) We use the story as an all-purpose interpretive lens—a means of clarifying experiences remote from school. We do this partly out of hunger for coherence, partly because, for complex reasons, history denies us other choices. Time now to remind ourselves of some essentials of that history—how the original faith in personal autonomy was instilled, why it survives, beating back challenges day by day, but in the process blocking access to genuinely inclusive truth: truth both about character and about community.

Chapter 9

HISTORY: THE FATE OF AUTONOMY

*T*he sole self that matters is that which is self-begotten.

External, impersonal factors, such as money and status (or their opposites), are irrelevant to true identity.

Independence, not profit and wealth, is the supreme value.

At no moment in the new nation's first century did economic reality or community life unambiguously support these as the ruling beliefs of the culture. To women and slaves— the majority of the population—the principles were obviously inapposite. Nor was slavery a phenomenon of the margins; millions knew what it meant and how it compromised American ideals; a half-million died in the war that finally brought it to an end. The principles of self-begottenness had equally small bearing on the lives of the industrial workers who were already being sweated, in the opening decades of the nineteenth century, by "slopshop entrepreneurs" in New

York and elsewhere. The true foundation of many proud affirmations of personal sovereignty and many high-minded rejec-
tions of dog-eat-dog moneygrubbing lay in the American "artisan
republic," and that republic—as the historian Sean Wilentz
writes—"disintegrated in the late 1820s." In every post-1800
impulse to invoke individualistic independence as a universal,
in short, elements of wish-fulfillment were present.

But the impulse proved to be inexpungible, partly because of the clarity of the ideal inspiring it, partly because
much that was unforgettable in the American past supported
the ideal. In the beginning community life did indeed center
on meetings in which participants represented themselves
alone, and spoke as equals. Getting a living did entail, for the
majority, mastering recognizable, identifiable competencies
and skills. Methods and pacing of work were largely self-
determined. Bettering one's land and dwelling by personal
effort was feasible. The relative sameness of resource or
income—much remarked on by foreign observers—did tend
to check the placing of people above or below each other
(such placing necessarily assigns significance to an impersonal order of value).

And promoting the causes of personal equality and independence ranked, for many, as a moral obligation. Virtue
opposed attempts to institute hierarchies; vice allowed the
claims of the social order to precede those of individual human beings. The attack on taxation without representation,
begun as a denial only of the authority of parent nation over
colony, quickly widened into an assault on subordination
itself. If colonist and Englishman were equal, it followed that
citizens must behave to each other as unconditioned equals,
no exceptions, not for elected delegates and representatives,
not for the rich, not for persons of "dignity." People were

not their positions; people were their natural selves. According to the dream, America would remain eternally a place wherein, as Bernard Bailyn puts it in *The Ideological Origins of the American Revolution*, "the status of men flow[s] from their achievements and from their personal qualities, not from distinctions ascribed to them at birth. . . ." Only where "there [is] this defiance, this refusal to truckle, this distrust of all authority, political or social, [can] institutions express human aspirations, not crush them."

In 1776 freeholders in one Virginia town instructed their delegates to the provincial congress to remember that "your constituents are neither guided nor ever will be influenced by that slavish maxim in politics 'that . . . the supreme power of the state . . . must in all cases be obeyed.' " The state was people; people were their natural selves. A Pennsylvania pamphleteer argued in the same year that differences in wealth should be reckoned as immaterial accidents. Money in the colonies signifies only that one person has been on the scene longer than the next (long enough to experience some land appreciation); no reason for wealth to "obtain the same degree of influence here which it does in old countries." People were not their fortunes; people were their natural selves.

A national theme arising out of this past—these gestures of defiance—was that building a better world than any hitherto known required that each person maintain a sense of independence of the past, of social identity, of authority in the large. And neither the inexorable movement away from the artisan republic, nor the haunting of the American imagination by slavery, weakened the hold of this theme on the public mind.

Enthusiasm for autonomous men and women—energetic, self-sufficient people in love with true openness and capable of producing personhood out of individual action, daring, talent, sweat—welled up in talk and writing. Noah Webster saluted the multi-gifted American—"husbandman in summer and mechanic in winter," fabricator of "a variety of utensils ... such as will answer his purpose," and "in some measure an artist" in the bargain. In 1841 Emerson smilingly hailed the "sturdy lad from New Hampshire or Vermont" who refuses to be "installed in an office" and instead "tries all the professions," "*teams it, farms it*, peddles, keeps a school, preaches, edits a newspaper, goes to Congress, buys a township ... and always, like a cat, falls on his feet. . . ." Popular culture and high culture shared an absorption with heroes driven by passion for variousness and the will to unconditionedness.

And politicos who knew no better than to speak up in favor of restrictive, enmeshing social definitions of value— "order and degree"—were doomed. Federalist aristos interested in re-creating a deference society were thrown out of office. Jeffersonian agrarians who succeeded them were prevented from imposing policies that would have set limits on individualistic, speculative energy and ambition. From the earliest colonial days, people short of privileges found that, in the expanding society, they could create new situations to the west in which they themselves might become distributors of privilege.

And many who were ambitious rose, providing support of a kind—through their self-made prosperity—for faith in the survival of individualism and personal sovereignty. In the mid-nineteenth century, according to the labor historian Herbert Gutman, "so many successful manufacturers who had begun as workers walked the streets [of Paterson, New Jersey] that it is not hard to believe that others less successful or just starting out on the lower rungs of the occupational mobility ladder could be convinced by personal knowledge that 'hard work' resulted in spectacular material and social improvement." When rates of ascent slowed and mobility took the form mainly of a step toward home ownership or the purchase of a piece of farmland to be worked part time, the sense of individual achievement remained strong. In mid-nineteenth-century Newburyport, Massachusetts, according to another historian, "laborers ... had abundant evidence that self-improvement was possible. To practice the virtues exalted by the mobility creed rarely brought middle class status to the laborer, or even to his children. But hard work and incessant economy did bring tangible rewards—money in the bank, a house to call his own, a new sense of security and dignity." Citizens who lift their levels of confidence and self-esteem by their own individual action rise above rank; they know the substance of autonomy from inside.

What they know isn't demonstrably what the majority of workers know—loggers, sailors, coalminers, farmhands, slaves; the totalizing habit of reading the universal in every anecdote of ascent derides truth rather than serves it. But in order for ideals and fantasies to thrive, experience need not confirm them in every particular, or obliterate every contradiction and tension. In mid-nineteenth-century America a time remained in memory when the artisan republic had possessed more than mythy substance. There was evidence, furthermore, that opportunity could be seized by the ambitious and industrious. And it was undeniable, after all, that the nation had begun with a rejection of constituted authority.

In their interaction these elements created dispositions of mind and feeling disturbing to visitors from abroad—carpers about American manners, spokespersons for an alien, chartered world in which rank was character. But the faultfinders were blinkered; they observed an uppitiness and missed an achievement: the emergence of people in number who *believed* they could compose their own nature and destiny, *believed* they knew how to pierce through externals to the human essence. Independent individualism in its purity might be far to seek—but Americans of many conditions imagined the country to be bringing to birth social arrangements under which identity would owe nothing to extraneous standards and orders. They saw their fellows as people who would make up their own being, rising freely, freely falling, exploring and testing themselves. Americans on this view were meant to be their abilities, not their stations; they were meant to be their strength, resiliency, fairness, trustworthiness, reliability; they were meant to be their plain unpretentious straightforward democratic natures; they were meant to be their delight in the cleansing winds of absolute independence.

In more than one respect that vision edged closer to reality in the nation's second century than in its first. Slavery was officially banished; officially, women became equals. But when this is said, it needs to be added that on many fronts the beleaguerment of the ideals of autonomy and independence steadily worsened from the mid-nineteenth century to the present. Patriotic rhetoric together with school instruction deemphasizes the social and economic change that has separated the country ever more irrevocably from its mythological past. When notice is paid to the national transformation, emphasis falls on wealth, opportunities, and rising living standards, not upon the developing discontinuities. Worship of independence remained mandatory, but the emerging structure of work and community life required sacrifices of independence (as traditionally understood). And it wasn't possible to view those sacrifices solely as selfless responses to necessity. Those who exacted the sacrifices ultimately compensated the theoretical victims at wage rates that cast the transaction in a less imposing light—made it appear a calculated swap of independence for comfort, luxury, life-possibility.

Hindsight avers that the situation called for some sorting out of underlying contradictions. An effort to reconceive the idealized values of the past in contemporary terms—a salvage operation of a sort—might have provided the value of independence with a solid footing in life as actually lived, and eased the extravagantly self-mythologizing compulsion. But who had leisure for and experience at adjusting conceptual systems to the flow of time? Much that was happening to the nation, including the formation of a deskilled working class, had happened elsewhere, earlier, in Europe; special circumstances—special blessings—helped conceal the resemblances. And in some sectors of the culture battles were fought—a hundred years of labor strife—to reclaim the dignity of work and workers. Elsewhere the emerging imperial middle scrambled to invent defensive gestures and strategies on the march, as needed, persuading itself that social and economic transformation belonged to the surface and that the basic stuff of national character remained untouched. For some years now the perfervid restatement of classlessness as the American norm has ranked as the most politically respectable of those strategies.

The forces creating the need for strategies are well known: industrialization, the decline of the labor movement, and the rise of the consumer society. Omnicompetent artisans

and small farmers had reason to believe in their unconditionedness and self-sufficiency, but factory operatives in the
mass—"hands"—tended machines and gradually became
separated from traditional crafts. Hired or fired in number,
punching in and out by shift, laboring in lines, they were
viewed as component parts. Owners dealt with them as workforces, loyal or disloyal; putative creators of worker solidarity
thought in terms of class consciousness, present or absent;
bureaucratic inquirers envisaged statistical cohorts. (State
commissions and legislative committees were taking testimony about working conditions from "representative workingmen" as early as the 1860s; rates of industrialization
reached their peak between 1840 and 1865.) Groups came
to be treated as infinitely more consequential than unitary
selves.

And groups treated each other as though conscious of
hierarchies of power and uniformities of station. Hurry-up
bosses, time-study engineers, sweatshop misery, union check-
offs, strikes, lockouts, Pinkertons, mass layoffs intensified the
hostility that homogenizes We and They. Individual identities
were compressed into "interests." A body of progressive legislators, bureaucrats, and social workers commenced to behave as though responsible for protecting and ministering to
a citizenry floundering in tides of change. The emerging language of "caring" confirmed that unanticipated changes were
occurring in the "universal" culture of autonomy and independence.

But, as just indicated, the directions of change couldn't
easily be assessed as unambiguously good or bad. In a volume
on *The History of Violence in America* Phillip Taft and Philip
Ross argue that the nation's labor history was, arguably, "the
bloodiest and most violent ... of any industrial nation in the

world." But when it became evident that property owners in the United States could kill strikers with impunity, prudence sanely retreated, and the retreat opened a path toward labor-management bargains whose name was abundance; fearfully dangerous solidarity was exchanged for safe, atomistic prosperity. Superior to any hitherto known, the bargains were steadily sweetened, in some sectors, in the early decades of the twentieth century, by corporate liberalism; the well-being thus gained sowed the seeds of lifestyle individualism—autonomy in a new key.

From its beginnings the country had been a place of exceptional material plenty, but the new abundance of industrial production heightened the sense of empowerment flowing from good hope and expectation. Abundance focused minds on future prospects, discounted social identities existing here and now, implanted optimism about imminent changes in levels of buying power and comfort (at least for the children). Abundance underwrote the nuclear family, cutting generations loose from each other, and masking social *im*mobility. (Grandparents, parents, children, aunts, uncles, and cousins sharing a domicile confront commonalities—social identities that remain constant over decades; nuclear families, locked in private aspirations, shrug off such identities.)

And abundance shaped the consumer society. Mass production of goods and services necessitated the manufacture of wants, and as marketing techniques improved, producers became skilled at presenting new products as new identities, intimating that individuality and independence are consumer goods. "Self" flourished—identity born, that is, in individual ambition, in aspirations for one's children, and most especially in desires and tastes. The objects people coveted—Chevy pickup, Morgan horse, sport-fishing gear, electronic keyboard, Nike shoes—reflected uniquely personal values and expertise; shoppers' worlds were their own.

What is more, now as before, leaders were elected, and possession of the vote was not the fruit of bitter struggle. In Europe populations were divided by denials of the franchise; struggling to end or prolong the division, each side grew self-conscious; before universal suffrage was achieved, universally shared values disappeared. In America white males at every level were enfranchised—no hiving off, at the ballot box, of the money and management hierarchy from "hands," no Election Day barriers between empowered and impotent. In nations where attaining the vote became a cause, party affiliation and voting behavior were predictable, consistent, class-controlled, impersonal. In this country fickleness was the rule. Americans constantly shifted allegiance and, from the time of the Whigs under Thurlow Weed to that of the Republicans under Reagan and Bush, rejected the notion that a political party could own them as a body for even half a generation.

In political talk, furthermore, personal readings of candidates' character ("What's he like as a person?") continued to shape opinion. The theme of true identity lived on; in concert with the equalizing ballot and shared abundance, it softened class boundaries developing out of the new economic structures. Common assumption insisted that voters and candidates alike were their real natures, not their public labels; politics was loose and pliant, hospitable to the personal will—an arena in which "independents" could stand forth as sole authorities upon themselves.

On their face, the political and socioeconomic arrangements seemed providential: increasing comfort for the majority, continuing prospects of self-realization. Thanks to abundance, personal wills ranged the malls, selecting and enjoying gratifications and distractions on a scale once unimaginable. The grand labor-management bargains that had made homeowners and car owners of skill-stripped factory and office workers were, to be sure, deals between unequals. The strong offered them to the weak only after teaching the weak hard lessons about vulnerability and powerlessness. Resentment at those lessons created at least one moment of extraordinary collective solidarity—the great sitdown strikes of the late 1930s—and still blazes forth in the American institution of talkback. (See Chapter 12.)

But over the years memory recast the lessons in a manner strengthening the conviction that on both sides choice had shaped the bargains—free choice, choice that remained open to the very present. Abundance had not required the total sacrifice of independence, said pride; it entailed no cringing consent to subordination, no shaming compromise of individuality. Hence no need existed to rethink the meanings of independence in the industrial or post-industrial age.

Nevertheless there was the need just mentioned for defensive gestures and strategies—means of confirming the continuing vigor of individualistic independence, ways of quietly demonstrating that no one had been bullied, no one had sold out. Some met this need in movie houses, their days made by entertainment featuring unintimidated selves. Others found individual strength by spurning the franchise, thereby asserting the insignificance of Establishment-sponsored election games. More than a few put the all-knowing, big-brotherly community in its place through the bravado of prejudice, racial and ethnic. (Intransigent bias and individualistic independence learned early, in America, to disguise themselves as each other.)

Strain and pressure were often evident. A spirit clearly wedded to optimism and never sustainedly mutinous would yet turn edgy, touchy—slipping into anomalous mistrust of self or society. Balkiness or sullenness abruptly jostled sunniness and content. Moments occurred when it seemed that in some psyches independence led a double life: one life arising from hope and plenty, another from fear of servility. The psychological dynamics were unplottable; only the underlying need—for *American* styles of behavior, for frequent assurance of the indestructibility of the uncowed self—was plain.

It bears repeating that the behavior that met the need, although sometimes perverse or mean, was seldom if ever threatening; the sense of fact bridled the eruptive will. Farm mortgages were foreclosed, plants shut down, malls built and abandoned, Medicare rules amended, billion-dollar bombers approved, mass transit canceled—and few failed to grasp that, on these fronts, the single self lacked potency. In contemporary culture personal survival demanded tactful, deferential readiness to negotiate with the superior force of governmental and other collectives; any nascent resentment was curbed by self-reminders that the deals and bargains of American life—lifestyle, the vote, the continuing possibility of ascent—are enviable. The task was to balance pleasure and self-respect—to relish both new shoes and standing tall.

Help toward that goal came whenever evidence appeared that could be interpreted as cautionary to, or diminishing of, The System: signs and warnings that defiance was not dead and The System was not infallible or invulnerable. Help came through acts of displacement that enabled dislike of collectives to express itself fiercely but harmlessly, without trace of sedition. Help came from moralizing upsurges that detached one or another event or person from the neutral amorphousness of things-as-they-are, creating sealed-off cases suitable for stern judgment. (The bringing of verdicts on the high-placed affirms not only the surveillance responsibilities of citizens but their capacity to interrupt the operations of any machine in the name of character, trust, right relationships between individuals.) And regularly there were enlivening experiences of identification with solitary agonists who dared to pit unitary being—the resources of the single self (as entrepreneur, airman, athlete, politico, soldier)—against the potentially oppressive weight of the organized, multifarious other.

In the twentieth century the classic act of displacement long centered on Red Russia. Functioning until recently as a distant boil that draws off infection from the world at hand, Red Russia allowed American enthusiasm for individualistic independence and autonomy to be voiced both passionately and innocuously (innocuously if regarded from a narrowly nationalistic perspective). No local power structure could be confused with the target; ferocity against Marxist totalitarianism established as though incidentally that the standard for assessing the state of autonomy in America derived no longer from this country's past but from the Russian present. Pre-*glasnost* Russia: people frightened of their shadow; mobs suckered by Big Brother with lies about workers-of-the-world; empty shops; brutal cops; trips to Siberia. Foreign observers nonplussed by anti-communist fury at every level of American society tended to miss the strategic function—the usefulness of redbaiting as a means by which the people as a whole ran, in an as-if, half-conscious fashion, their own masked, harmless campaigns against "Washington." (*Try pushing us around the Russian way. Just try.*)

Similar warnings are issued when, with media aid, the public takes up symbolic moral or criminal cases construed as humbling to The System. Figures of greed, breakers of trust—Boeskys, Milkens, Helmsleys—are soberly weighed. A serviceable patch of corporate or governmental arrogance or incompetence is held under television scrutiny for weeks. Shock is voiced; Congress is concerned; workers "win" sixty days' notice of plant closings; acquiescing to public pressure, the General Accounting Office outlaws thousand-dollar toilet seats.

The feelings engaged run from moral outrage to contempt, and the upsurges set the plain decent common sense of autonomous democratic selves over against the supersubtlety, avarice, or ridiculousness of the managers. *Our values are still intact. It's the big boys who are in trouble.*

Most poignant, perhaps, is public participation in the agons of latter-day Emersonian hero-individualists—votaries of total unconditionedness. In the late twentieth century agonists are not expected to arrive chaste at the amphitheater. Those who fight for the solitary self may well be persons who, to the very eve of battle, are seen as dutifully obedient to the collective. Their past is irrelevant: if they are gripped by the ineradicable spirit of individualistic independence, if they break out and defy the hierarchy, the nation will be moved.

Once in recent days an agonist proved to be—astonishingly—a former national enemy. Because it was ignorant of the power of the person, the Kremlin had outlawed change and declared reform unthinkable. But Mikhail Gorbachev—an isolato, a communist, yes, but an individual first, a smiling, lively, birthmarked believer in the potent self—succeeded in turning the Kremlin around. America was moved. More typically, the agonists are *echt* Americans. Because the auto industry was ignorant of the power of the person, it pronounced Chrysler dead. But Lee Iacocca—an isolato, a businessman, yes, but an individual first, a believer in the potent self—turned the company around. Or again: because the community of the knowing was ignorant of the power of the person, it declared America to be a helpless giant, doomed to endless humiliation by martial Marxists in banana republics and meddling solons on Capitol Hill and screaming religious fanatics overseas. But Oliver North—yet another isolato, a soldier, yes, but an individual first, a believer in the potent self—turned the situation around. As these and similar figures enter their agons, excitement mounts—delight in combative presences, people hell-bent to go one on one with The System.

North's orders specified he was to free the hostages and aid the Contras. Squarely in his path loomed a mighty Them, bristling with amendments, conventions, protocols, standard operating procedures, chains of command that constrain the healthy impulse of the individual to declare that none but he or she can be the authority on themselves. A bit player in a basement office, North slightly resembled—at the moment he received his orders—Lt. Andrew S. Rowan who, in the Spanish-American War, was made bearer of a "message to Garcia" by the President.

Like Rowan (as described by Elbert Hubbard in a beloved turn-of-the-century newspaper piece), North suppressed dumb questions: "Was I hired for that? . . . What's the matter with Charlie doing it? . . . Is there any hurry?" He was unafflicted with what Hubbard termed "this incapacity for independent action . . . this infirmity of will, this unwillingness to cheerfully catch hold and lift." North lifted. He didn't tell himself he would be ruined if he failed to offer two dozen ranking officials a chance to sign off on a course of action. He didn't tell himself that, compared with august, constituted presences such as the U.S. Secretary of State and the U.S. Secretary of Defense, he was a nothing. He didn't tell himself that it was inconceivable for a marine officer of barely field grade to function simultaneously as substitute-President, diplomat, banker, spy, thief, bureaucratic fixer, entrepreneur— *echt* omni man.

He believed he could team it, farm it, peddle, buy, sell, govern. He believed he had the right to preach sermons on his political and religious views to the high muckety-muck Congressmen and Senators arrayed before him in ascending tiers of desks—sermons they were meant never in their lives to forget. And he believed, further, that when his day was finished, he would land on his feet like a cat, set up a new stand in a new town, and prosper.

And as his confidence came across—his sense of the rightness of autonomy, the exhilaration of it—strong feeling flooded toward the man from every corner of the country. The feeling could not last. Implicit in it was no endorsement of a policy, no judgment on reserved rights, the Boland amendment, the Reagan Presidency, the ghastly ordeal of the hostages, or the future of Latin America. Nor did those who raised their chins pugnaciously with "Ollie" somehow believe his example would annul the past, opening a path on which henceforth omnicompetent men and women would once again stand tall as Crockett and Boone, free of encumbrance and ascribed condition. The public recognized North as a rare bird, as they recognized rareness in Lindbergh, taking off against advice in bad weather, as they recognize it in Gorbie, bareheaded, shaking hands in American city streets, or in foulmouthed, impudent Iacocca (to Henry Ford: "You don't know how the fuck we made the money"), able single-handedly to turn a dead company around. The public was without illusions concerning claims to absolute autonomy. A farmboy and ex-con named David Allen Coe earned a fortune with a country song called "Take This Job and Shove It," but as the song climbed the charts, bumper stickers quickly appeared in the Southwest bearing a sober, conditioned answer: I WISH I HAD A JOB TO SHOVE.

Yet fact doesn't cancel rapture in the ideal as it resurfaces, can't quash the inner conviction that respecting—more than respecting, prizing, even for an instant *loving*—the solitary figure struggling for his independence is a civic duty. Hailing Ollie, the public declared not that he was correct or wise or a happy omen, but that Independence is still recognized and honored when it appears, that it arouses profound gratitude and satisfaction, that it possesses releasing power, and that it proves we are what we were. Right or wrong, absurd or heroic, Oliver North will do for a day as an emblem of the permanence of the real self, of the true identity that survives intimidation. Absorbed in his performance, observing The System scrambling awkwardly to meet his charge, the soul of independence is refreshed and history shrivels.

Identifying with Colonel North's defiance is a different action from remorselessly judging Ivan Boesky (assured that the moral issues of the world of finance involve nothing except permissible and impermissible degrees of greed). Both actions are different from spurning the vote or vilifying Jews or African-Americans. Choices among gestures of independence vary according to educational level and aren't equally eligible for highminded chastisement. More to the present point, each action belongs to the same configuration of self-deception to which faith in American classlessness belongs.

In the public mindset the gestures coalesce; they are in some sense inseparable from each other. Together they clear a space for protest on behalf of the primacy of the individual; they retrieve self at least momentarily from conditionedness; they encourage self to utter the words hallowed by autonomy faith: I am what I am, I am myself alone.

No curtly dismissive assessment of this clung-to faith—no indictment of it as the fruit of brainwashing—is tenable. Electric, charged with joy in the active will, the faith is often cursed by mindlessness, timorousness, plain hate—but it remains a major if paradox-ridden source of the improvisational freedom, irreverence, and spontaneity of American life and manners. Had it lost its vitality, the great politico-moral advances of our time would have been unthinkable. The nation managed to unfreeze the hierarchies imposed by racism and sexism only because heroism was still free to speak for true identity. (African-Americans are not their stations but their natural, individual selves; women are not their stations but their natural, individual selves.) Conceivably this freedom will expire if the imagination of unconditionedness is replaced with conventional class consciousness.

Good sense seeks no such end. It understands the interdependency of the ideal of classlessness, the long dream of independence, and the potentially elevating intuition that abundance is not enough. Good sense believes only that intelligent realism about class conditioning can aid the search for better means of fostering individualistic independence for all. Its goal is to insure the survival of a value by disentangling the value from fustian, and providing it with a foundation securer than lies and illusions.

Why pursue that goal? Partly because the for-profit oversimplifications of officialdom and commerce demand correction—but for other reasons as well. One is that insistence on classlessness falsifies history—in particular the history of group solidarity among workers. Had genuine labor solidarity been achieved in America, it might have laid a firmer foundation for commitments to personal autonomy and natural selves than lifestyle consumerism provides; the failure to achieve solidarity was in part a result of intimidation by terror. That past deserves remembering not solely out of piety but because a powerful truth converges in its lens: American hostility to knowledge of class and its workings has positive as well as negative dimensions, is not traceable to brainwashing, deserves better than to be targeted for conventional intellectual demolition; yet only by moving beyond the hostility, acknowledging the profound social changes that have complicated the ideal of independence, can we prevent trivialization of the ideal.

Another reason for rejecting the myth of classlessness is that the myth belittles successful passages of collaborative struggle in our past that are immensely more useful in dramatizing the might of ordinary men and women than Oliver North's self-serving days in the witness chair. I have in mind the inspiring episode that began on a bus in Montgomery, Alabama in 1955 and comprised 381 days of brave, brilliant, collaborative effort by thousands who, because they refused to deny their social identity, placed themselves in position to transform it. Well before Dr. King was chosen to command them, Montgomeryites were risking their lives, achieving rich individual fulfillment by working together, in disciplined teams, to improve each other's chance of realizing the truly independent self. The lesson of their victory, somewhat obscured by idolatry of their courageous leader, is that solidarity brightens the prospect for full individuality, and that the myth of classlessness—if uncontested—thwarts solidarity.

Still more important reasons for countering the myth arise from its impact on social psychology, public policy, and the life of creative minds. Although visions of the unconditioned self are liberating, the culture of democracy can survive without them. But it badly needs clear thinking about why people are placed as they are, how hierarchy is established and sustained, what positions in a class or status system actually signify. The lie that the society is all one—no levels, no powerfully limiting socioeconomic influences, a single body of citizens fused into an imperial middle—sets obstacles in the path of this clarity. The standard fantasies—*Class is a racket. Class is temporary. Class is occupation. Class is psychogenic. I did it my way. Each has access to all*, and the rest—have power and authority on their side (as does every notion that promotes satisfaction with things as they are). Because they strengthen confidence that, by virtue of nationality, Americans possess a special instinct for justice and fairness and an inner check against seigneurial conceit and haughtiness, the standard fantasies become a cornerstone of national pride.

But it does not follow from either point that, in the social development of individuals—the growth of capacity for companionability, the building of a foundation for social feelings tougher and richer than those of Have-A-Nice-Day—the myth plays a positive role. And it continues to function ruinously in the political arena, corrupting policy and debate, subverting serious political involvement and commitment wherever the latter seek to breathe.

This book thus far has concentrated on two aspects of the national attachment to the idea of the classless society:

the nature of the rationalizations that help to suppress consciousness of social differences, and the links between the rationalizations and media, entertainment, "equal educational opportunity," and history. Ahead lie the tasks of examining the myth's influence on political life in America, and of inquiring into resources available to those who mean to contend against that influence. The purpose is, first, to show how the influence operates on policy formation and, second, to characterize the attitudes, perspectives, and self-conceptions of those who in the recent past have done most to combat the influence. The assumption is that the myth of classlessness should be seen not only as a fixed, far-reaching, abstract structure of falsification handed to us from the past, but as a force in immediate decision-making against which resistance is urgently necessary. The search for levers capable of moving a frozen society needs to go forward on many fronts; on each of these fronts knowledge of how faith in classlessness affects public action, as well as private thought and feeling—particularly the body of feeling properly described as American vanity—is indispensable.

· *Part IV* ·

PUBLIC MINDS AND PRIVATE CONDUCT

·

Chapter 10

PUBLIC POLICY IN THE CLASSLESS STATE

What exactly does it mean to say that American public policy is everywhere infected with the influence of the myth of classlessness? It means that publicly financed options, advantages, and programs theoretically available to all are in fact restricted, by official rulings and by the social distribution of civic and other competencies, to a favored few. It means that social problems resulting in significant measure from government-sanctioned or administered inequities are metamorphosed into incidents in a grand struggle between good and evil—a struggle represented by "realists" as lying beyond government intervention. It means that an endless succession of program failures is blamed on "bureaucracy," instead of upon the obscurantist, legislatively consecrated definitions of problems with which bureaucracy is obliged to work. It means the spread of doubt, by the media, concerning the feasibility of rational management of public affairs. It means a descent by leaders into sentimental stoicism.

And it means the threat of near-total governmental surrender to socioeconomic crisis.

In every situation American public policy displays obligatory solicitude for the figure who has haunted these pages: the unconditioned individual, the person of will and ambition who builds identity solely from a moral core within and is in no significant measure socially determined. The beliefs underlying the solicitude are by now entirely familiar: individualistic choosing is the definitively American activity; citizens who don't participate in this central activity are found only on the margins of society; the differences between nonchoosers (the tiny minority) and choosers (the often embattled but still vast majority) are moral and characterological in nature, not socioeconomic. Talk and decisions based on these beliefs can be moderate or extreme; the tone is adjusted to economic and political weather. The state negotiates accords between champions of social provision and proponents of strict observance of personal responsibility and self-discipline; its own official discourse includes both panegyric on moral individuals and the unconditioned self, and arguments for federal help for the helpless.

But no turn of political weather—no "emergency," no "problem"—ever lifts from the state the burden that the myth of classlessness imposes upon it: that of insisting on the representativeness—the place at center stage—of the unconditioned American. And from this felt obligation stem the consequences just named. Commitment to the legend of the average American as unfettered chooser makes it impossible for the state to take adequate account of the complex actualities of a class society. More than once in recent times the resulting state-administered class injustice has been not less than appalling in its human cost. And the longer-range consequences—the undermining of belief in the possibility of reasoned collective action—are yet more serious. Structured authority comes to be viewed as incapable of defending the interests of decency and fairness; suspicion mounts that nothing on earth can long stand in the path of brutality and fraud; a sense of futility and impotence becomes the norm.

By far the worst recent episode of state-administered class injustice occurred during the Vietnam war. Between America's formal entry into the war, in 1964, and the taking of Saigon by Viet Cong troops in 1973, 27 million men came of draft age; 60 percent of them—about 16 million—escaped military service. Then as now it was often assumed that the majority of the escapees were draft evaders who took flight to Canada, Sweden, or elsewhere; actually only about 3 percent of the 16 million (570,000) were draft offenders. Nine out of ten escapees missed the war because officially deferred, exempted, or disqualified on grounds of mental or physical handicap; most of these were sons of the imperial middle. And the inequities were directly traceable to the myth of classlessness—the influence ultimately responsible for official wrongheadedness in dealings with the draftee population.

During the war and after, the inequities were underpublicized; no formal hearings were held. But the story was no secret. General officers observing rifle companies rotating out of the line noted the absence of a cross section of American youth. "In the average rifle company," wrote General S. L. A. Marshall, "the strength was 50% composed of Negroes, Southwestern Mexicans, Puerto Ricans, Guamanians, Nisei, and so on." A Chicago-based wartime study, unofficial but methodologically sound, established that "youths from neighborhoods with low educational levels [were] four times as likely

to die in Vietnam as youths from better-educated neighborhoods." A Wisconsin Congressman polled a randomly se-
lected one hundred inductees from his district—unlucky
youngsters, that is, who had missed out on deferments—and
found that *all* belonged to families with incomes under
$5,000. A Harvard *Crimson* editor learned—also by polling
—that of the 1,200 members of the class of 1970, only two
went to Vietnam. The Defense Department was apprised that
a quarter of the Americans killed in combat in 1965 were
blacks, and subsequently took steps to alter the racial balance
of casualties; no action was ever taken to alter the class balance of casualties.

Social commentators with middle class bases were re-
marking, as early as 1972, that they "had never known a single
family that had lost a son in Vietnam, or indeed, one with a
son wounded, missing in action, or held prisoner of war."
And by the mid-Seventies article writers had begun describing
Vietnam explicitly as a "class war."

The author of one of the first of these articles, James
Fallows, contrasted—in shame—his behavior on the morning
of his draft physical examination, in 1969, with that of a
contingent of "white proles" arriving after him for the same
examination: "the boys from Chelsea, thick, dark-haired
young men. . . ." A Harvard senior in good health, Fallows had
a low draft number, wanted desperately to secure a physical
deferment, and had been carefully coached on how to obtain
one. He knew, for example, that his "normal weight was close
to the cutoff point for an 'underweight' disqualification"; he
knew—because a doctor had told him—that he could help
himself by faking a fainting spell. At the physical exam he
made a try at fainting; he also persuaded an orderly to weigh
him a second time after the man first registered his weight

at two pounds above the cutoff point (120 lbs.); he told an examining physician, untruthfully, that he had lately been contemplating suicide. The combination worked; the physician "wrote 'unqualified' on my folder." The boys from Chelsea, on the other hand, just out of high school, were completely uninformed. "It had clearly never occurred to them," Fallows wrote, "that there might be a way around the draft. They walked through the examination lines like so many cattle off to slaughter."

Not astonishing. The small army of so-called "draft counselors" that provided Fallows and millions of others with expert guidance on draft loopholes and exam-beating was usually located in university settings to which high school grads with jobs lacked easy access. (In the early Vietnam years every university student received automatic deferment.) The panels of draft attorneys who prepared appeals of draft board decisions worked cheap—fees of from $200 to $1,000—and promised results, but they were hard to reach by anyone lacking money and experience at seeking legal aid. (The head of the Los Angeles panel told reporters that "any kid with money can absolutely stay out of the Army—with 100% certainty.")

Doctors, dentists, and psychiatrists who became specialists in draft avoidance labored chiefly for the advantaged. "The people we saw," said one doctor, "were all middle class. [The others] just never thought of going for professional help." Low-income youngsters knew nothing about the more exotic modes of help available to would-be draft avoiders—such as the infamous "order of call" defense employed by thousands. This scheme involved mathematical investigation of draft board records in search of evidence that boards had called up registrants out of the order specified by their lottery numbers; one mathematician formed a corporation called Draft Research Associates to run the investigations, charging each client $250. As for less exotic ways out (the National Guard, the reserves): these modes of service, in which "duty" often consisted of golf and bridge, were class preserves. "Reservists and guardsmen were better connected, better educated, more affluent, and whiter than their peers in the active forces," and minorities knew better than to apply.

What lay behind the multitude of imperial middle ploys, scams, hideouts? Mainly the ignorance of officialdom. Officials didn't know (or didn't know it mattered) that some young men are taught the location, name, and nature of the levers of power, and that some are not, and that class holds the key to this difference. They didn't know (or didn't know it mattered) that some young men are taught that city hall can't be fought, and that some are taught ways of outwitting city hall instead of fighting or capitulating, and that class holds the key to this difference. They didn't know (or didn't know it mattered) that, for these and related reasons, trusting a theoretically uniform physical examination or uniform appeals process to insure equality of treatment was naive.

Doubtless officials and draft board members were aware, at some level, that differences existed between college-educated youngsters and "the boys from Chelsea" who entered the labor market straight from high school. But the awareness lacked edge and clarity. Rationalizations multiplied: *Eighteen-year-olds who aren't in college could be if they chose—and might be tomorrow (the education system is open). . . . Eighteen-year-olds who are in college attend by virtue of merit (the education system is meritocratic). . . . Eighteen-year-olds who aren't in college are, very probably, either indolent or obstreperous or both, hence are properly regarded as moral inferiors. . . .* Officialdom simply did not grasp that failure to heed class-based differences in access to knowledge about how to beat the draft could lead to a disastrous imbalance in the distribution of wartime suffering.

And, to judge from official Selective Service papers, the root cause of the mistakes was obsession with the average American as individualistic chooser. Public statements and testimony by the Service's head, General Lewis B. Hershey, argued that the draft system could be made distinctively American by stressing individualistic choice; they implied that potential draftees who were in a position to make choices constituted the majority. "The psychology of granting wide choice under pressure to take action," Selective Service declared in 1965, "is the American or indirect way of achieving what is done by direction in foreign countries where choice is not permitted." It's also the best way, because "an individual generally applies himself better to something he has decided to do rather than something he has been told to do." Our system exerts " 'pressurized guidance' to encourage young people to enter and remain in study, in critical occupations, and in other activities in the national health, safety and interest. . . ." The statement added: "From the individual's viewpoint, he is standing in a room which has been made uncomfortably warm. Several doors are open, but they all lead to various forms of recognized, patriotic service to the Nation. Some accept the alternatives gladly—some with reluctance. The consequence is approximately the same. . . ."

Who were the individuals in the "uncomfortably warm" room? In introducing them the policy statement described a recent shift of opinion regarding occupational deferments—an emerging belief that "for the mentally qualified man there is a special order of patriotism other than service in uniform.... For the man having the capacity, dedicated service as a civilian in such fields as engineering, the sciences and teaching constitutes the ultimate in their expression of patriotism." Clearly the individuals in the warm room were people who benefited from this new perspective on deferment—"mentally qualified" professionals or pre-professionals in training who could express their patriotism best by choosing to stay out of uniform.

But both the policy statement and later Selective Service pronouncements spoke as though the world of "pressurized guidance" familiar to those individuals was the same as that known by youth generally. When officials used such phrases as "young people" and "the young man," they were referring to persons in position to choose occupational deferments, and imagining the pre-professional as Everyman. Describing the psychology of potential draftees, Selective Service wrote: "The young man registers at age 18 and pressure begins to force his choice. He does not have the inhibitions that a philosophy of universal service in uniform would engender. The door is open for him as a student to qualify if capable in a skill badly needed by his nation. He has many choices and he is prodded to make a decision."

Fusing "the young man" about to make a choice with young men who knew nothing of choices—the high school boys James Fallows perceived as cattlelike—made the job of assuring fair treatment for the whole draftee population look easy. Selective Service planners knew that all the choosers in the warm room weren't the same, morally speaking. But, they said, we apply *uniform* pressure, seeing to it that everyone who chooses to be occupationally deferred—advantage-seekers, whiners, the selfless—faces "the threat of loss of deferment" throughout college, graduate school, and thereafter.

In the planners' view, intense vigilance over those who chose deferment would guarantee the fairness of the system as a whole.

This was worse than nonsense. The planners' absorption with choosers left their system vulnerable to the scams that involved millions. It made them assume that fairness for 483,000 choice-making, deferred professionals and pre-professionals—one thirtieth of those who escaped the draft —meant fairness to all. And beyond question, their mistakes flowed directly from commitment to the muddy, unexamined substance of Americanism: the middle as all, equal opportunity guaranteed, social differences as moral differences in disguise. Because the state was in thrall to the myth of classlessness, "the great bulk of ... Americans deeply scarred by Vietnam were those already economically, socially, and educationally disadvantaged"; the waging of the dirty war was left to the boys from Chelsea and to blacks.

Unusual both because statistically verifiable and because based on articulated assumptions, this particular episode of class injustice is in few other respects atypical. Decisions of state taken in fields remote from that of wartime manpower policy show the influence of the same habits of oversimplification and the same ruling assumptions and themes— choice, the individual, the single sector construed as the social whole. Peacetime tax exemptions parallel wartime draft exemptions, with inequities arising because one group within the population—comparable to that composed of pre-professional potential draftees in the warm room—is seen not as a group but as the whole.

Consider, for example, the treatment of mortgage interest. Officialdom distributes a huge subsidy to homeowners;

the subsidy bears no trace of the stigma attached, say, to food stamps. The implicit justification is that home ownership is universal and socially stabilizing, and that those not now sharing the benefit could share it if they chose. In reality, because of the nature of the urban housing stock, an enormous number of working class urban families can never make that choice, and are excluded from the benefit. But their inability is often viewed as a characterological defect (renters don't *save*), and, in any case, the habit of deleting the factor of social difference renders the families in question relatively invisible (like the boys from Chelsea). When the matter of urban housing needs is raised, the state pleads lack of funds, and the head of state produces one-liners. (After reading that the city of New York paid $37,000 to support a family in a welfare hotel for a year, President Reagan remarked: "I wonder why somebody doesn't build them a house for $37,000.")

The links between the myth of classlessness and the major areas of class injustice—housing, education, health care, Social Security taxes, the court system, and the rest—warrant meticulous inquiry. And the methods of inquiry themselves demand the same. Conventional approaches to social injustice—not excluding the so-called multi-leveled approach taken, a generation ago, during the War on Poverty —often emerge as misdirected efforts to seal off problems that are in fact beyond enclosure. "Nutrition problems" are dealt with in isolation from "literacy problems," and vice versa; dropout problems, teen pregnancy problems, homeless problems, jobless problems, drug problems—all are fenced and bounded, in contempt not only of their obvious interrelationships but of the direct bearing on each of tax-supported arrangements and bonanzas in other sectors of the population. And inevitably the frustrations arising from the "failures" of programs conceived in these terms leads to the practice of moralizing, minoritizing, and biologizing socio-economic realities.

The effect of the latter practice is to transform difficult but comprehensible problems into mysteries involving dark forces and defying rational search for solutions. The lack of decent rental housing, in cities, for working class and lower middle class families, is in no small measure the result of the bestowal of federal largesse on some classes and the with-holding of it from others. And this philanthropy involves much more than mortgage interest, of course. Five hundred billion is spent to bail out well-heeled savings and loan bank-ers, while pieties about the "inexorable laws of the free mar-ket" are preached to *bodega* owners in bankruptcy and to foreclosed family farmers. And at state and city levels huge handouts are distributed to Sears and other corporations in the form of "tax increment financing" arrangements under which inner city locations are abandoned and glossy new corporate headquarters in suburbs are subsidized with public funds.

But when housing shortages are set in a moral context, the class aspect of the problem disappears, memories of class bailouts fade, and mystification enters. The mortgage interest tax exemption and related tax breaks become rewards for the virtuous and circumspect; the absence of a mortgage is subtly converted into a sign of recklessness; the collapse of urban housing becomes entangled with the problem of the nature of man; government can only turn up its hands.

Moral and even metaphysical entanglements—distrac-tions leading minds away from clear issues of class advantage into murky jungles of casuistry—figure regularly in the his-tory of American public policy planning. Well before the turn of the last century, one historian writes, the prevailing elite ideology identified "the fundamental division in American society not [as that] between rich and poor, but [as] between industrious and idle, virtuous and vicious, community-minded and selfish." This conception of difference played a role in shaping the first functional equivalent, in America, of an old age and disability pension system—the benefits that were paid to a million and a half Civil War veterans and their survivors. According to Ann Shola Orloff, writing on "The Political Origins of America's Belated Welfare State," Civil War pension benefits "flowed primarily to members of the middle class and the upper strata of the working class, rather than to the neediest Americans." From the time of those first pensions to the present, when, as Theda Skocpol argues, "social security" for "deserving workers" is bifurcated from "welfare" for "barely deserving poor people," the distinction between the decent and indecent, virtuous and vile, has dogged American social provision. But lately the theorists of dark forces have grown more aggressive in attributing program failures to moral corruption, and in dismissing the notion that improved public policy could ever succeed at the task of moderating inequity.

In support of that notion a large arsenal of weapons is deployed, including the weapon of pseudo-science—the branch represented by inventors and promoters of what is termed the "pathology of poverty." These promoters purport to provide objective, penetrating, social-scientific accounts of things as they humanly are. The manner of the descriptions is candid and unflinching; a claim is made for the respect awarded those whose thankless task is to face the worst. But the substance induces feelings of despair—a sense that the crises of the age are biologically foreordained and that utopians alone dream of abating them through human intervention. Who among us knows the answer to Evil?

Among the best-known promoters of the pathological fallacy is Edward C. Banfield, a professor of government at Harvard and head of President Nixon's Task Force on Cities. In *The Unheavenly City* (1970) Professor Banfield presents himself as "a social scientist [thinking] about the problems of cities in the light of scholarly findings." ("Facts are facts, however unpleasant.") His thesis is that American cities are in ruins because the underclass individual isn't normal—is mentally ill, pathologically sick:

> [He] lives from moment to moment . . . Impulse governs his behavior, either because he cannot discipline himself to sacrifice a present for a future satisfaction or because he has no sense of the future. He is therefore radically improvident: whatever he cannot consume immediately he considers valueless. His bodily needs (especially for sex) and his taste for "action" take precedence over everything else—and certainly over any work routine. He works only as he must to stay alive and drifts from one unskilled job to another, taking no interest in the work . . . He feels no attachment to community, neighbors, or friends (he has companions, not friends), resents all authority (for example, that of policemen, social workers, teachers, landlords, employers), and is apt to think that he has been "railroaded" and to want to "get even" . . . Much of [his] violence is probably more an expression of mental illness than of class culture.

Here he is, the unconditioned American individual, in new guise. *I am what I am. I am myself alone.* In accounts

such as Banfield's the man of the underclass is a person cross-
ing an open field, making free choices as he goes. He can
decide in favor of the long view—decide, say, to follow the
example of his father (a Bell Labs engineer) and develop a
science hobby in junior high (taking over the basement rumpus room for a lab); decide to develop a research focus on
robotics under the guidance of Mr. Herman, the brilliant
young senior high chem department chair (Herman has already had two GE Young Scientist finalists); decide at Cal
Tech that space robotics is where he wants to go; decide to
take the Lockheed/NASA post-doc offer, etc., etc.

Or he can decide to "live from moment to moment" in
West Harlem, opting to work as a steerer-lookout for his
dealing brother at age nine and ten, opting to heist car bat-
teries at twelve, opting to drop out at thirteen, opting thereafter for dealing and pimping. Life is options. It's up to him
whether he respects authority or despises it; immaterial that
authority from his first encounter with it assumed that he
would despise it. It's up to him—to his free choice—whether
to work at a skilled or an unskilled job, whether to study and
train or drift and steal.

If a street kid opts for joblessness when straight before
him lies the rumpus room/robotics/Cal Tech option, what can
this mean except that moral sickness has gripped his soul?

An effective labor movement might have done much to
counter the claim that unemployed people, such as Banfield's
inner city alienated, are sick; it could also, through its backing,
provide activist legislators and policymakers with reason for
seeing themselves not as isolated do-gooders but as representatives answerable to lively, demanding, expectant constituencies. But owing to factors ranging from right-to-work
laws to a century of Red-baiting, no such labor movement

exists. Nor does any political party with a disposition to challenge the assumption that social problems are, in essence, problems of morality and pathology. Perceiving themselves as omni-entities, American political parties express horror at the prospect of "polarization" of business and labor; they compete with each other for business alms ("Republicans represent corporate oil; Democrats, independent oil; Republicans represent commercial finance; Democrats, the savings and loan associations"); they deny that class exists.

In the course of their careers few policymakers at work today have heard even the beginnings of a serious public discussion, by political leaders with unfickle constituencies, of the impact of the American class system. What they have heard, almost ceaselessly, is criticism—murmured or shouted—of "government interference" in the affairs of individuals, and denunciations of "special interest lobbies." (Equal rage is directed—democratically—at oil lobbies and lobbies for coalminers.) And the result is that critics and criticized alike arrive—by different methods of reckoning—at quasi-agreement that such interference is not only unavailing but at least partly responsible for nourishing the dark forces.

In the past quarter-century federal initiatives in the areas of poverty and welfare have joined federal regulation of business as chief targets of opportunity for enemies of "government interference." No initiative in the welfare and poverty areas was ever shaped on the basis of accurate understanding of the pertinent class differences in education, expectation, housing, and family structure. And, not surprisingly, most of the initiatives passed swiftly through a cycle beginning in optimism and ending in chaos. Office of Economic Opportunity programs were condemned early for waste, unfairness, and "coddling," and later for worsening the situations they were intended to rectify. ("Poverty programs cause poverty," as Sidney Blumenthal mockingly summarized the standard indictment in *The Rise of the Counter-Establishment*, 1986.)

As for expanded welfare programs: first a famous white paper discovered that their unanticipated consequence was the destruction of the black family, then the dark force theorists developed the point into an indictment of government itself. Charles Murray, the Reagan Administration's welfare theorist, claimed in 1983 that the "liberal ascendancy" was blind to the real cause of anguish in Harlem and comparable communities. The real cause is government; the new welfare programs are actually responsible for the moral collapse of the poor; all such programs must go. Let government be mindful henceforth of the consequences of ignoring the ineluctable individuality of each of its citizens. Let the nation ponder the costs of deleting the moral substance from "conditions" and pretending that life is a "social problem" soluble by technical means. Let men and women remember the truth of original sin—most especially the sins of working people and the poor.

Viewed in these terms, inequity—even inequity traceable to specific, misconceived government action in the past—takes on the status of nature: appears weighty and irreversible. The elements of the basic situation are these: there are people of light and people of darkness, and although the former may send their rays—their hope—toward the latter, they can do no more. Nor can government itself; it cannot function as the locus of purposive action on the side of sound human values. As awareness of this basic situation takes hold, a sense of powerlessness and self-elevating moral stoicism settles over the capitols and statehouses—disbelief that the intricate interrelationships among problems can or perhaps should be clarified, doubt that alliances necessary to create public support for legislative solutions can or perhaps should be forged. Vying for the crown of *a*politicality, leaders tell themselves and their constituents that hope resides nowhere save in individual impulses of benevolence—the kindness of one person to the next. And *we* the imperial middle are the kind; the capital of benevolence, as of light itself, is in our sole charge.

In late August, at public and private lakeside summer camps around the country, American counselors and youngsters participate in a ceremony with vague East Indian roots: Wishboat Night. Campers set adrift on the water small paper boats to which lighted candles are affixed; watching the rows of tiny flames—points of light—edge out from shore, flare up and disappear, self-consumed, in the darkness, campers sing and say their goodbyes. A farewell ceremony, innocent, touching, sweet. The tone of points-of-light politics bears a distinct resemblance to the tone of Wishboat Night. Hope trembles, flickers, dies, and a note of regret prevails. Little can be done; soon our brief season will end; let it be remembered, however, that, on the edge of darkness, we were concerned.

The voice sending the moral message—let us be kind, let us be gentle—sounds other themes as well: time-honored themes of individualism and choice. And these are invoked as energizing and optimistic. The people of darkness are exhorted to recover their identities as individualistic choosers. Choose not to do drugs. (Just Say No.) Choose an elementary or secondary public school for your children (through one's own individual acts one can solve the "education problem");

a federal program called CHOICE is in place to enable individual citizens to become school-choosers. Choose to become, like ourselves, individual, autonomous points of light. Shed meanness, shed ignorance, let our light—our goodness—be your guide.

An expansive self-approval combined with imperial middle self-pity for moral responsibilities bravely borne blights these entreaties. And the implicit withdrawal from politics—from the labor of defining commonalities of interest, forming new coalitions, framing new bargains—is absolute. The steady disparagement of government carries a promise: officialdom won't soon again be driven by overconfidence into an error as huge as that which made Vietnam a high school boys' war. But the note of surrender is unmistakable: government as government gives up on itself.

The language that needs desperately to be spoken—the only language in which the interconnectedness of bad schools, bad housing, bad nutrition, and horrific family life can be grasped, and strong but hidden joint interests can be defined—is the indispensable language of class, and that language is proscribed. And the proscription is, finally, most devastating because, as I said, it extends the influence of the myth of classlessness well beyond the mere enforcement of consent to inequity. By legitimizing the claims of the middle as sole moral exemplar, it lifts all restraints on ruling class ego. And by depriving government of its own power to imagine a complex response, it insures that government can never be equal to complex problems. State and citizenry alike stand forth as victims of that deprivation because both are robbed of the only resource on which either can afford for long to rely: the resource of *mind*.

Chapter 11

CLASSLESSNESS AND THE STRUGGLE FOR MIND

What the mind at its best can do is challenge class response and class vanity—scrutinize both for reductiveness and sentimentality, penetrate the delusions that are spawned by top-down, moralizing points of view. In addition the mind can establish coherent relationships among the elements that converge in actual human response (character, personal belief, class, national past), seeing to it that none claims or is awarded automatic dominance. And beyond this the mind can tackle the thorny moral and political issues arising as societies redefine their responsibility for the contingencies that face individuals.

The mind can do these things *if* its basic capital is intact, namely awareness that sound social understanding is inevitably, irreducibly complex.

In a class society committed to the denial of class, this awareness is difficult to sustain. Calling the myth of class-lessness larcenous is, indeed, no empty figure of speech. The myth blunts the feeling for the contradictoriness of experience, steals the capacity to suspend judgment and look before and after. Because of its oversimplifying power, pieces of the truth are constantly being mistaken for the whole, connections between each part and every other part are neglected, and immodesty and self-righteousness take command.

All this comes clear, though, only through examination of specific episodes: passages of the past wherein mind struggles against myth, wages war against reductiveness, with consequences both for politics and for the self that can be gauged. The field of conflict is the history of ideas, and reaching it entails retreating a step from contemporary experience. But the engagements are not theoretic; more than one has touched real lives counted in the tens of millions.

On toward the middle of this century a resurgence of social, political, and moral thought occurred in America. Orthodoxies that had formed among the educated classes in the late Thirties and early Forties underwent revision. History was reconceived. Thinkers engaged in the reconception saw themselves as laying the foundation for a richer political culture. Their work stands to this day as a powerfully reasoned effort to supplant the myth of classlessness with understanding of the complex interaction of class and character—understanding useful to a community attempting to think and feel its way forward to clearer social vision.

But the generation that succeeded the intellectuals in question had a different self-concept and a different project. It transformed the elders' themes, readying them, as it emerged, for the mind of the Eighties, and producing the set of sociopolitical oversimplifications that came to be called neoconservatism. (Several who participated in the transformation were Reagan-era fixtures.) Within barely a decade the idea of the classless society was reconsecrated; soon after came a troubling return of belief in dark forces.

The leaders of the original struggle on behalf of complexity—the elders—were Robert Merton, Richard Hofstadter, and Lionel Trilling (a sociologist, a historian, and a *littérateur*); they shared the goal of emancipating American liberalism from naïveté. In the Forties and Fifties, employing different methods and tools, investigating different materials (historical movements, novels and poems, social structure), each published critiques of simplistic moralism. Hofstadter was bent on overturning idealized versions of the Populist Crusade. Trilling was concerned to clarify the moral standard he found in the living novelist he admired most (E. M. Forster). He located that novelist's distinction in his witty brief against the mind that believes "the order of human affairs owes it a simple logic: good is good and bad is bad"—the mind that understands "the moods of optimism and pessimism" but can neither name nor understand "the mood that is the response to good-and-evil." Merton, for his part, supplied a theoretical analysis of social structure which inquired into the mental landscape of the underclass.

All three writers were critics of the propagandistic stereotypes which, in their time, sought either to heroicize or villainize American working people. By one stereotype the latter were metamorphosed into proletarian demigods, hailed as the saving "masses" ("Masses are never pessimistic," wrote Michael Gold. "Masses are never sterile. Masses are never far from earth. Masses are never far from heaven.... Masses are simple, strong and sure"). The competing stereotype, which gained strength as unemployment deepened in the Depression, represented workers—especially jobless workers—as mentally ill.

Hostile to both stereotypes, Trilling, Hofstadter, and Merton were committed liberals, selectively influenced by Marx. They were aware of the inapplicability of Marxian economic concepts to advanced industrial nations, but could not delete from consciousness the convictions that had drawn them to Marx in the first place. Their writing is bare of signs of impassivity in the face either of suffering or of destructive uses of the social wealth of the West. They were capable of anger at unintelligent, self-deceiving caring—"concern" that lacked vitality because encrusted in cliché and piety. They held that a liberalism lacking in critical self-consciousness, unwilling to confront the toughness of its moral and social task, blind to human reality, would in time be helpless to beat back totalitarian threats. And since, as Trilling pointed out in 1950, there was no chance that aid could come from American conservatism (that tradition was intellectually dead), he and the others would have to try to supply the criticism, from within.

But it would not be destructive criticism, would not sink into the righteous rage that leads some correctors of faults to demolish the structures they set out to repair. Functioning as a critic-from-within of liberalism would mean turning an unsparing light on weaknesses without gutting either one's own best self or the best selves of like minds. The talents required included both self-restraint and adeptness at handling double truths: truths about interdependencies of class and character.

Those gifts are well illustrated in the person of Stephen

Elwin, the hero of "The Other Margaret," a short story by Trilling that appeared in *Partisan Review* in 1945. Among the earliest attempts by a reflective critic of liberalism to use his urban experience as a means of revealing the contrarieties of liberal faith, the story follows Elwin, a publisher, through a routine urban day in which he and his wife encounter misbehavior on the part of several representatives of classes different from their own—members of the allegedly "simple, strong and sure masses." The encounters direct the hero's inner reflections and prepare him for the story's crisis, which is brought on by the misbehavior of the Elwin family's new black maid, the other Margaret of the title. (Elwin's daughter, a teenaged schoolgirl, is also named Margaret.)

The approach to the crisis begins before dinner, when Elwin's wife, patience gone, tells her husband and daughter that the new maid is a "nasty, mean person." The daughter objects, having learned at her progressive school that Negro domestic servants are exploited by the class to which she belongs. When she proceeds to argue, further, that the poor can't be held responsible for their acts, Elwin—to his own moderate surprise—interrupts. "Why not?" he asks, and his daughter explains, "Society didn't give her a chance.... She has a handicap. Because she's colored. She has to struggle so hard—against prejudice. It's so *hard* for her."

Cautiously, non-rhetorically, Elwin draws young Margaret's attention to family experiences—happy experiences—with an earlier black maid, proposing that handicaps are borne differently by different people and that moral behavior depends heavily on the individual human being's self-conception. The earlier black maid had had to borrow money from the Elwins and was still repaying it. Elwin's daughter insists that "she can't afford it"; Elwin, agreeing, adds that "she can't

afford not to," either, because "she needs to think of herself
. . . as a responsible person."

A few moments later there's an eruption: Margaret the
new maid gives notice abruptly to her employers, and then
smashes, seemingly by intention, a bit of pottery that Margaret
the daughter had made for her mother as a birthday present.
This event, together with Elwin's previous criticisms of the
talk of "prejudice" and "handicaps," begins young Margaret's
advance from cant.

"The Other Margaret" is a shade solemn in execution,
and (for us) outdated in idiom; it is not a masterwork of
fiction. It is, however, a suggestive portrait of a liberal wres-
tling with himself. It shows us a mind determined not to
dodge the difficulties inherent in any autarchic concept of
either societal or personal responsibility. Frustrated by those
difficulties, Elwin has been sorting them out for himself, and
takes no satisfaction in his effort to do the same for his daughter. (Satisfaction isn't the hallmark of "the mood that is the
response to good-and-evil.") When, toward the end, he declares himself, his tone is rueful: "Had he been truly the wise
man he wanted to be, he would have been able to explain,
to Margaret and himself, the nature of the double truth. As
much as Margaret, he believed that 'society is responsible.'
He believed the other truth too [the truth of personal re-
sponsibility]."

But it is a declaration, and it is commensurate with the
events of Elwin's day. Those events—ranging from a patch
of Jew-baiting witnessed by his wife to a bus conductor's
harshness to a child—bring pointed reminders that individual
failures to achieve standards of personal responsibility are in
part a function of lack of advantage (the "gentle rearing and
the good education that made a man like Stephen Elwin answerable for all his actions"). The same events confirm that

mean deeds are committed by whites and blacks alike and demand to be considered in the light of the circumstances generating the need for acts of resistance and rebellion; the circumstance that counts most is that low-income blacks are, in the main, bullied and powerless. As "The Other Margaret" closes in on the conduct of one member of that class—and upon one kind of liberal platitude—none of these reminders is forgotten. And as a result the unflamboyant assertion of belief in a "double truth" has strength and weight. To some readers at the time the story seemed like the beginning of a national awakening from a social and cultural trance.

An exactly parallel effort—an effort to subject cant to cold-eyed scrutiny without obstructing potential moral progress—animated Hofstadter's and Merton's writing. And resemblances exist between the authorial personas of both scholars and the character Trilling named Stephen Elwin.

The moral oversimplification that troubled Hofstadter arose, as noted, in contemporary idealizations of populism and progressivism as crusades, by the uncorrupt, to "bring back a kind of morality and civic purity that was … believed to have been lost." Be realistic, Hofstadter counseled himself and others in *The Age of Reform* (1955); consider the facts of class, of class interest, of class myopia. The evidence reveals that populists were often parochial and sometimes anti-Semitic. Then, as ever, heartland innocence had a kinky streak. Writers and thinkers who signed on with progressivism from above, on the other hand, were vulnerable to fantasy about the interest of "the masses of people" in "logic and principle." The moral status of populism and progressivism, like that of other popular reform movements, was "ambiguous," and fools alone found them wholly credible as crusades.

And yet the movements do not warrant scorn or dismissal. "Humanitarianism, courage, and vision" figured in them from beginning to end. What's more, "within the limited framework of the reforms that were possible without structural alterations in the American social and economic system, the [reform movements] did accomplish something...." If we're to avoid replacing mere lamebrained puffery with mere bombshell exposé, we need to work our way in closer to the reformist psyche, tracing relations between character and class, spelling out the etiology of behavior. One reason for the reformers' excessive revulsion at trusts, bosses, and other evils was that "the religious institutions of Protestantism provided no mechanism to process, drain off, and externalize the sense of guilt." Another was that "American political traditions provided no strong native tradition of conservatism to reconcile men to evils that could not easily be disposed of." Evangelical Protestantism induced a conception of responsibility according to which, wrote Hofstadter, "everyone was in some very serious sense responsible for everything," and self-deception entered because the typical person in whom the sense of guilt and shame was quickened had no intention of making "any basic changes in a society in which he was so typically a prosperous and respectable figure."

As the historian shifted focus to character and character formation, he stepped forth as a writer who, like Trilling, was aiming at sustained responsiveness to a multi-leveled social and moral reality. Once again the promise was an end to platitudinous assessments of behavior and issues—and to nonsense about classlessness. Advising against idolatry of characters who are "ready to be convinced that the country [is] thoroughly wicked" but aren't prepared to make personal sacrifices to correct the situation, Hofstadter nevertheless insisted that such idolatry isn't totally invalidating or crippling.

The reformist sensibility was naïve and bigoted at one class level, and, at a different level, deficient in self-knowledge and self-irony. But at both levels the sensibility commanded respect as a humanizing, broadening, and healing force whose influence helped to save America from becoming "nothing but a jungle." Our goal, as readers of our past, shouldn't be to exchange sentimentality for indifference but rather to press ourselves for comprehension of the double truths within our own moral natures.

It was partly from Robert Merton's *Social Theory and Social Structure* (1949) that Hofstadter learned how to write about corruption-obsessed reformers from a viewpoint not of superiority to public-spirited concern but of anxiety about the moral dimness that can accompany—and disable—that concern. (Merton had brought off this feat in a treatment of latent functions of political machines.) But Merton spoke more directly than either Trilling or Hofstadter to the issue of class and character, addressing himself to villainizers of working people instead of to their heroicizers. In the late Thirties and early Forties earnest attention was being paid to academicians and others who had begun arraigning the Depression-battered jobless, on pseudo-biological grounds, for weakness, lack of self-control, and collapse into deviant or criminal behavior. (A typical arraignment was E. Wight Bakke's *The Unemployed Worker*, which appeared in 1940.) In the manner of Trilling, Merton rehearsed the varieties of meanness and failure targeted by these voices of disillusionment. He acknowledged that case histories often establish that episodes of defiance among the alienated and penniless —"dramatic kinds of illicit adaptation"—are "linked with patterns of discipline and socialization in the family." But then, in the manner of Hofstadter moving sympathetically inside

the grievances of populist farmers and analyzing their sys-
temic roots, Merton explained in class terms why it was a
mistake to link deviancy solely with individual failure to control "imperious biological drives." His explanation ranks to
this day as the best account of anomie in the American context.

It began with an analysis of the uniqueness of that context. Here was a culture teaching that everyone should "strive
for the same lofty goals," that "seeming failure is but a way-
station to ultimate success," and that "genuine failure consists
only in the lessening or withdrawal of ambition." Yet, Merton
said, the same culture "restricts or completely closes access
to approved modes of reaching those goals" to people at the
bottom. Those shut off often know nothing about the "structural sources" of their plight. They've been teased away, many
of them, from the solidarities that might ease their pain, been
instructed to "identify themselves, not with their compeers,
but with those at the top...." They can see no substance
in—no reasonable place in their daily lives for—virtues and
habits considered by others to warrant thoroughgoing respect. Given these realities, what kind of expectations of the
poor or of low-income minorities are realistic? And does it
make sense to posit biological causes for deviancy? "When
poverty and associated disadvantages ... are linked with a
cultural emphasis on pecuniary success as a dominant goal,
high rates of criminal behavior are the normal outcome."

Neither here nor elsewhere in Merton's work is the principle of personal accountability denied, or a hint offered that
crime ceases to be criminal if committed by somebody on
the bottom rung. And there is no tolerance of evasion or
euphemism. Deviancy swarms in its variousness, bearing
plain labels in his pages: "psychotics, autists, pariahs, outcasts,
vagrants, vagabonds, tramps, chronic drunkards and drug ad-

dicts." But the writer drives himself against overpersonalization of behavior. His book anatomizes disillusionment with the masses in a way that clarifies why the disillusionment itself is a species of blindness to the workings of "the social and economic system." And there are blunt words for the racism lurking in biological accountings of the so-called underclass ("the anti-Negro charges which are not patently false are only speciously true").

Obviously these three writers differed as to which aspect of the religion of classlessness causes greatest harm. Trilling and to a lesser degree Hofstadter were primarily disturbed by the phenomenon of sentimentalization: the guilt-inspired refusal to acknowledge that all human behavior has personal as well as social roots, and that blanket laudation of any group, on any ground, is at once stupid and hypocritical. Merton began elsewhere, with a critique of judgmentalism: the tendency to discount every influence on behavior except that of character. But all three writers were pressing for a fuller, more flexible accounting of social and moral difference than that which the reigning mythology would allow. Each clearly believed that exposing strains and contradictions in fundamental values—sympathy, generosity, hope—not only served truth but ultimately strengthened the values. Often acerb, seldom suffering fools gladly, they nevertheless would not descend, when engaged in dissecting fatuity, into mockery of the feelings of compassion, within themselves and others, that ennoble great struggles against injustice. Nor were they morally self-vaunting. Their vision had limits but their social tone was humane, bare of taunting and derision.

What happened to their effort? It was beaten back, as I said, by a generation that couldn't bear complexity—couldn't meet the obligations that criticism of the myth of classlessness

imposed on men and women of mind. The critique was tra-
duced, turned inside out, transformed into what it was never
intended to be: an attack on classes below the middle. The
humane social tone disappeared, and with it went the foundation of a memorably intelligent attempt to correct American naïveté about class.

The works in which Merton, Hofstadter, and Trilling laid
out their critique were all in print by 1955. Within a decade
their versions both of the underclass and of liberal faith were
sharply revised—by younger writers who began intellectual
life as their disciples. And the process continued into the
Eighties, wherein politically influential works regularly invoked the names and language of the elders—the critics-from-
within—while espousing positions the elders could not
approve. Books and authors by the score, hundreds of issues
of weekly, monthly, and quarterly journals of opinion, played
a role in the transformation. The chapter of the history of
ideas was written in a period of social upheaval every phase
of which had as much impact on thinkers and writers as the
Depression and Cold War had upon Merton, Hofstadter, and
Trilling. Some observers have seen the key events as direct
results of mean-spiritedness and ungenerosity in the successor generation; too few have grasped that their pivotal significance lay in the sponsored re-emergence of the mythology
of classlessness.

One key text, Norman Podhoretz's "My Negro Problem—and Ours"—appeared in *Commentary* in 1963. The
young editor had been Trilling's student at Columbia, and he
emulated his teacher in "My Negro Problem" by drawing on
his own urban experience in assessing liberalism. But there
were differences. Dispensing with the distancing, softening
screen of fiction that locates imagined problems in imagined

worlds, Podhoretz wrote his piece as an autobiographical essay set in a cityscape of hard facts. It opened with a description of the author's puzzlement when, as he was growing up in Brooklyn, in the Thirties, he saw in print the claim that "all Negroes were persecuted." The puzzlement arose from his experience of being "repeatedly beaten up, robbed, and in general hated, terrorized, and humiliated" by blacks. They "were supposed to be persecuted [but] it was the Negroes who were doing the only persecuting I knew about—and doing it, moreover, to *me*.... What could it mean ... to say that they were badly off and that we were more fortunate?"

The center of "My Negro Problem—and Ours" consists of several pages of incidents of violent real-life bullying by blacks. Podhoretz remembers himself one day angering a "surly Negro boy" named Quentin—who had "a very dark, very cruel, very Oriental-looking face"—by answering in class a question the Negro boy had failed to answer. Later that day Quentin and his little brother, "who is carrying a baseball bat and wearing a grin of malicious anticipation," come after Podhoretz, "in front of my own house," and the bat, wielded by Quentin, "crashes colored lights into my head. The next thing I know, my mother and sister are standing over me, both of them hysterical. My sister—she who was later to join the 'progressive' youth organization—is shouting for the police and screaming imprecations at those dirty little black bastards. They take me upstairs, the doctor comes, the police come. I tell them that the boy who did it was a stranger, that he had been trying to get money from me. They do not believe me, but I am too scared to give them Quentin's name."

After several similar accounts of murderous violence, Podhoretz asserts that he still feels hatred for blacks, that he believes most white Americans are "for whatever reason, it no longer matters ... twisted and sick in our feelings about Negroes," and that he despairs of "the present push toward integration." He acknowledges that his feelings of hatred must be overcome, alluding to "that clichéd proposition of liberal thought," namely that "it is *wrong* for a man to suffer because of the color of his skin." And in his closing sentence he imagines himself one day having strength enough to give his daughter "my blessing" if she wants to marry a Negro.

In "My Negro Problem" people at the bottom are not seen as members of a class *and* as individuals, as Trilling sees them. They are seen as powerful—not, as in "The Other Margaret," simultaneously powerless and capable of enraging gestures of rebellion. The situation of the class vis-à-vis that of the rest of the population becomes enviable (Negroes are "the very embodiment of the values of the street—free, independent, reckless, brave, masculine, erotic ... not giving a damn for anyone or anything"). The bottom of society is evoked as all of a piece, not made up of individuals variously capable of maintaining standards of personal responsibility, but almost uniformly violent, persecutory, and black. As for liberal faith: it is no longer cliché-ridden *and* morally energizing; it is purely hypocritical. "Everywhere we look today in the North," Podhoretz wrote, we find "liberals with no previous personal experience of Negroes ... discovering that their abstract commitment to the cause of Negro rights will not stand the test of a direct confrontation," and "fleeing in droves to the suburbs."

Over the years the themes became increasingly familiar: concern for the underclass is sentimental (exaggerates both the worth of the people and the seriousness of their wound), and liberalism itself is a dogmatic faith ("abstract," inelastic, terrified of fact). But the themes counted for less than the writer's own self-concept. It was a self-concept in which reflectiveness was imagined as a process of shucking off, and derision and judgmentalism become norms. The elder put himself forward as someone aware that without wisdom, judgments of others are empty, and that wisdom, because modest, seldom recognizes itself; his approach to understanding led through complexity and the elaboration of links between character and class; qualification, irony, and self-doubt were basic elements of his thought. The successor, proudly hardnosed, envisaged himself as a specialist in unadorned shocking fact that told its own story plain. His name for double truth was tedium.

Stanley Elkins, a pupil of Hofstadter's and the author of *Slavery* (1959), spoke in a quieter voice than Podhoretz's, and on matters more distant, but delivered a yet more jolting message: moral outrage at slavery in nineteenth-century America was groundless. Like Podhoretz, Elkins began with a perspective framed in its basics by the critique of liberalism from within. (The crucial text for him was Hofstadter's *The Age of Reform*.) *Slavery*, a sensation when it appeared and a work with which scholars in the field must still cope, developed an argument in which mid-nineteenth century and earlier enemies of slavery corresponded to the enemies of trusts and bosses in Hofstadter's study of progressivism. The book echoed Hofstadter in tracing the moral extremism of the reformist sensibility to Protestant guilt. But to his reformers Hofstadter had granted courage and a measure of effectiveness; he also treated the problems and conditions they protested as worthy of public outrage. Elkins was stonier. He represented the abolitionists as "morally implacable" prigs, nowhere acknowledged that they were effective (were unquestionably responsible, that is, for emancipation), and raised doubt about the seriousness of the problem they were addressing.

It was the doubt about slavery as evil that made *Slavery* a cultural incident. Elkins claimed that it was wrongheaded to reject, automatically, the stereotype of the full-grown Negro slave in America as less than human, as a lazy, lying, silly, dependent child—a Sambo. Historians should seek a "way of dealing with the Sambo picture, some formula for taking it seriously." The formula at which Elkins arrived found the Sambo picture to have been essentially correct; it was no insulting myth but a fair likeness of the reality. The conclusion that followed—a shaky conclusion—was that the abolitionists who whipped themselves into frenzy about the crushed humanity of the slaves as a class were caught in fantasy, victims of abstract moral absolutism and foolish anti-institutionalism. The first fact about Sambo wasn't that he belonged to a class but that he was not very smart.

Had they been sensible, therefore, the abolitionists would have been more tolerant of slavery as an institution. They would have adopted a gradualist strategy, respecting the rights and sensibilities of slaveholders, and treating slavery as less appalling than their ferocious damnation-dealing had made it out to be. Sambo was Sambo, was he not? How could he have known what was happening to him? The intellectual should have sought "a relationship to the humane slaveholder which need not inevitably have been one of 'friendly sympathy' but would certainly have had to be one of responsibility, of sensitivity to his requirements." A possible model might have been "the hard-bitten Englishman Wilberforce, who, for all his merciless campaigning for emancipation, could still be appalled at a premature proposal in the House of Commons to do away with the whip as the badge of authority in the West Indies."

The subjects of Elkins' *Slavery* and Podhoretz's "My Negro Problem" stand worlds apart, but in each work a younger writer sheds an elder's concern for complexity and contrariety. Each writer signals that the response of outrage to injustice ("merciless" campaigning for emancipation, "premature" doing away with whippings) is inappropriate. Each indicts as abstract and destructive the feelings of shame at the condition of the underclass which his elder would not criticize without first honoring as essentially humane. Each disallows the claims of the underclass to the status of an oppressed group, edges toward mockery of humanitarianism, and reads double truths out of the record, and taunts from above.

At no time in the Sixties and Seventies was the generation of critics-from-within forgotten, but memory of what it stood for grew steadily fainter. By the late Sixties it seemed almost as though sociologists and others who cited them in their work had no grasp whatever of their attitudes or purpose. Edward C. Banfield, for instance—the Harvard professor of government who denounced the underclass as pathological in *The Unheavenly City* (1970)—spoke of Merton and Trilling as though their minds were akin to his. Similar misreadings turn up in the work of Charles Murray, the welfare theorist who recommended abolition of welfare. In *Losing Ground* (1984) Murray studied thirty years of federal programs, and alluded often to the work of Robert Merton. But each of the reductive themes first sounded in the Podhoretz-Elkins generation of the late Fifties and early Sixties has a prominent place in his book.

Murray's analysis of those who cried *mea culpa* about poverty in the Sixties strikes the note of controlled contempt heard in Elkins' dismissal of those who cried *mea culpa* about slavery. White anti-poverty activists are accused of "moral agonizing" and "guilt." Quotation marks sneer at the "purely 'good' civil rights movement against the nasty southerners." Concern for the poor is defined as irrational and obsessive: "White confusion and guilt ... created what Moynihan has called 'a near obsessive concern to locate the "blame" for poverty, especially Negro poverty, on forces and institutions outside the community concerned.' "

All welfare programs fail because character is all and class is nothing—hence Murray's proposal to scrap "the entire federal welfare and income support structure for working-aged persons, including AFDC, Medicaid, Food Stamps, Unemployed Insurance, Worker's Compensation, subsidized housing, disability insurance, and the rest." And, as is well known, this proposal completed a cycle in the political arena. The concept of social inequity was rejected, and the new orthodoxy of Ronald Reagan and George Bush commenced speaking firmly on behalf of the old icon of classlessness. Reagan assumed a stance of doubt—of instant incredulity—when told of poverty and suffering. He observed that the Sunday newspaper listed thousands of jobs for which there were no takers, and that some homeless people slept on grates "by choice." Edwin Meese insisted that "some people are going to soup kitchens voluntarily ... because the food is free and that's easier than paying for it." The voice of political sophistication intimated that the sense of shame or of pity for the miserable and the unlucky reflected an absurd "passion of compassion" (as *The Public Interest* characterized it)—soft, emotional, Rousseauistic. Swiftly the thesis of dark forces returned, and the myth of classlessness reestablished its extraordinary hold on the national mind.

When viewed in the context of this recent political history, the work of Trilling, Hofstadter and Merton—its steady

consciousness of class influences on behavior—clearly qualifies as exemplary. Yet despite its evident superiority to the
villainizing and heroicizing mush that preceded it and the
stoniness that followed, it does have limitations. The critics
of liberalism were themselves excessively fixated on
morality—tended to assume that when the social causes of
moral or immoral behavior are understood, the basic substance of social reality is understood (and the absurdity of
the myth of classlessness is amply demonstrated). They
tended also to be over-convinced of the immaculateness of
their own moral universes. Stephen Elwin in "The Other Margaret" is a man mired in a master-servant relation that his
own Judeo-Christian tradition views as corrupting—yet Trilling presents him as a person "answerable for all his actions,"
who lives the ethical life as a free and unconditioned agent,
observes high standards of conduct and responds sympathetically to the difficulties and misfortunes of others. Equally
troubling, Trilling as storyteller assumes there's no need for
Elwin (or the reader) to hear the servant speak in her own
right, characterizing her actions, for the reason that all human
and moral worth in this situation resides unambiguously with
the master and his family.

A parallel kind of shut-in-ness afflicts Hofstadter. Assured
of the parochialism and meanness of Populists in the hinterland, he feels little compulsion to enter their minds—to shift
from the top-down perspective to a view allowing an immediate, particularized engagement with their way of thinking and feeling. Even Merton's pioneering attempt to
penetrate attitudes of the underclass is shadowed by a definition of virtue which, like Stephen Elwin's, provides a near-
blanket exemption from moral scrutiny to the whole of one
privileged class. The account of the "deviant" in *Social Theory
and Social Structure* nowhere raises the possibility that a

deviancy of the presumed normal may also warrant examination. (The law finds nothing criminally deviant, to be sure, in the levels of selfishness ratified by current distribution of opportunity and advantage—but behavior inoffensive to law can still be abhorrent to decency.)

What's missing, in short, is the voice from below—the voice that confronts subtle moral analysts with actualities of which they're oblivious. The struggle for mind is in one dimension a struggle against—against moral stereotypes—and the critics of liberalism fought it well. But it is also a struggle for—for patient attentiveness to the moment-to-moment realities of the interaction of class with class, and for comprehension of differences between "moral problems" as conceived from above, and the contradiction, crisis and chaos below as experienced by "working stiff types" and men and women on the margins.

Neither the character of the chaos nor the nature of its links with the myth of classlessness can be spelled out satisfactorily in orderly consecutive discourse. The chaos finds expression, typically, in wild gesture, uncontrollable hilarity, passionate song, sobs, screams—in the Basic English, that is, of the vibrant American arena of talkback. We cannot leave our subject until we have listened a little to the voices of talkback—to the critique of the myth of classlessness *from below*. It's when the imperial middle sees itself through the eyes of that critique that it draws nearest to the heart of its own fatuity.

▪ *Chapter 12* ▪

AMERICAN TALKBACK

I did it my way.
America: Love It or Leave It.
We're all equals here.
Whites, right! Blacks, get back!

*T*he language of talkback is uppity, rude, and (judged by conventional standards) uneducated. It's fluently spoken by certain rock and roll performers, stand-up comedians, film actors and directors, cartoonists and comic strip artists—but also intrudes into high art (particularly into documentary fiction and nonfiction). Talkback alludes often to well-known grievances. Inequality: the growth of vast discrepancies between the lives of the rich and poor. Favoritism: governmental solicitude for persons of means and unconcern for bottom dogs. Givebacks: the justice system selling, at prohibitive rates, legal rights originally awarded freely to all. Greed: operations transfers and plant closings displaying cavalier corporate disregard for hardships inflicted on workforces.

Typically, though, talkback artists bypass familiar conflicts of haves and have-nots, preferring to concentrate on cant and humbug unique to the allegedly classless society. A singer or comic will focus, directly or obliquely, on a bumper sticker or other slogan, allowing it to serve as a point of satiric reference. (The chosen slogan will be one that the educated understand to reflect the beliefs and limitations of a benighted class.) The talkback artist turns the slogan inside out, jams it with ironies, transforming it into a means of probing large issues of trust, of love of country, of friendship and fraternal feeling, of the tyranny of the bland.

Talkback asks both a certain height and a certain flexibility of its audience—alertness to the possibility that performances seen as mere entertainment can carry a potent charge. Listening well demands suspension of conventional senses of "the serious" and the intellectual. It also requires responsiveness to idioms wherein subtlety and coarseness are interdependent, and a renunciation of cultivated distaste for the raised, emphatic voice. The rewards aren't negligible: escape from decorous abstraction; entry into a world that's at once gross, steely and matchlessly energizing.

1. I Did it My Way.

"He is not a cockroach," came the quiet reply from the deep easy chair. De Niro's voice was calm.... "He is not a cockroach."

Stephen Bach, *Final Cut* (1985)

Late in 1978 the deal between United Artists and Martin Scorsese and Robert De Niro to produce a movie about Jake LaMotta, the fighter, appeared to be falling apart. Trying to save it, two UA studio executives and a producer paid a visit to the director and star at Scorsese's New York apartment. The UA executives, David Field and Stephen Bach, laid out management's concerns, which began with the script. They spoke of the obscenity level. ("There must be more *fucks* in this script than have actually taken place in the history of Hollywood.") They objected to some business specified for closeups. ("When I read in a script 'CLOSEUP on Jake La-Motta's erection as he pours ice water over it prior to the fight,' then," said Bach, "I think we're in the land of X.")

Most important in the UA mind was the conception of the primary character, Jake LaMotta. "It's this *man*," said David Field. "I don't know who wants to see a movie that begins with a man so angry, so ... choked with rage, that because his pregnant wife burns the steak, he slugs her to the kitchen floor and then kicks her in the abdomen.... Violence may be part of this man's life, demons of rage may be fucking up his head, but why should anyone stick around for the second reel?"

Both Scorsese and De Niro admitted that the script

needed repair, but Field pressed them harder. "It's not finally about the writer.... The problem is will anyone want to see *any* movie about such Neanderthal behavior? Can any writer make him more than what he seems in the scripts we've seen?" "Which is what?" Scorsese asked. Field's answer came swiftly: "A cockroach."

Into the silence that followed De Niro repeated the words that appear in the epigraph above: "He is *not* a cockroach."

The finished film, *Raging Bull*, created a character who did indeed confirm this assertion, and De Niro's contributions to the achievement were manifold. Although the star asked for no screenwriting credit, he (with Scorsese) appears to have been responsible for "the draft of *Raging Bull* that made Jake LaMotta human." And his performance was remarkable. The LaMotta it animates has moments of delicacy that set the character free from the demons of rage—briefly but affectingly, and without obtrusive underlining. In his car, for example, on a first date with the fragile-featured young woman he'll marry (she's played by Cathy Moriarty), the fighter moves his macho hand roughly toward her shoulder—and checks it in mid-course, with an odd, absently self-chiding grace that's beyond manners or tactics. During the couple's first lovemaking, LaMotta combines—in voice and movement—passion with tenderness that approaches reverence.

The scenes framing the story offer further views of recognizable humanness. Finished as a fighter, bloated and blasted, LaMotta is a cabaret curio, doing recitations before bored, unfriendly audiences. We watch him in a nightclub dressing room practicing his act ("I coulda had class ... I coulda been a contender": lines from the famous Brando speech in *On The Waterfront*). The memory work produces strains—and satisfactions. In the ring LaMotta was a performer, and in the nightclub turn he becomes a performer again. He also becomes, willy-nilly, a student, which is harder. Awkward in that role, yet not despising it, he simultaneously learns and chafes at learning. We feel the buildup in him of physical impatience at the unaccustomed labor—the vast relief of leaping up from practicing lines, casting away schoolwork for the freedom of a few seconds of self-exhorting, grunting, wind-expelling shadowboxing, hands and arms pumping with incredible velocity, the whole body hurled into physical expression. The figure that emerges is no tough softie, Hollywood-style, a champ turned poet; he's a human being in whom variegated currents flow—an "adult learner," a bum, a proud heart, a truant, an ordinary worker earning a dollar and trying to live on a little.

The ordinariness matters because it removes the fighter's demons from psychopathology and allows them to be read for what they are—heightened prototypes of common frustrations. LaMotta is caught like lesser countrymen in the dream of unconditionedness, the religion of success. Exceptional in many senses, powerful in craft, briefly rich and celebrated, he nevertheless believes all the standard public lies. He believes in hard work—punishingly hard work; in careers open to talents; in the right of the person who has made himself the best (and is committed unreservedly to remaining the best) to behave with proud independence; in that person's actual obligation to reject overtures from sly, dickering gatekeepers whose cynicism corrupts the system. A man of honor, an American straight arrow, LaMotta stands up for individual choice and unimpeded personal will. "He likes to do things his own way," says his brother, trying to explain LaMotta's intransigence to the gambler-gatekeepers who, determined to cut a deal with him, block his path to the title. "He wants to make it on his own."

He wants to and can't, because he doesn't own the levers, can't procure deferment from conditionedness. As he learns that the open society is in fact closed, for him, he does what many before him have done: takes out his frustration on those closest to him, allows the public lie to poison his personal life and the lives of those he's trusted and idealized. And it's at this point that talkback commences, turning its fury against the fraudulence of *I did it my way.*

LaMotta tries to do battle with cynicism, wrestles the gamblers who tell him the dream of independence is bunk. (You're "not going to get the title shot without us.") But the inevitability of the fix—the tank job, "the old flip flop"— keeps erupting in his head, racking him with suspicion. His wife, he tells himself, is selling him out to the gamblers. ("I saw you say hello." "Nothing. I said hello.") He charges his brother—his only friend—with sleeping with his wife. ("Did you? Did you fuck my wife?") Swiftly he's sealed into envenomed isolation.

At a different social level the problematics of personal freedom and personal virtue become material for meditation, but for Jake LaMotta as De Niro conceives him they issue in cruel, crazed, jealous fury. Talkback speaks in the actor's conception of the character. It goes straight to the roots of the man's fury in scene after scene, telling us that a human being suckered and cheated day after day in the work to which he gives passion and intensity and in which he excels has no choice except that of universal mistrust; he cannot end otherwise than by despising his own pride and seeking to destroy himself.

The scene of would-be self-destruction in *Raging Bull*

is appalling. The fighter's wife is gone—and his children, fame, honor, career, proud physicality. In solitary confinement, jailed on a false charge of pimping for a minor, LaMotta curses his gullibility—and tries to crush it. With all the force in his being, alternately sobbing and howling like Lear at his stupidity, he hammers his body against confinement, pounding fists and forehead against stone, screaming his protest at the lie of Fair Fight. And, through the combination of the monumentality of his rage and the essential ordinariness of its sources, he becomes a voice for the voiceless—a countervoice to mythy individualistic independence wherever it deceives and anesthetizes. Bearing witness to the victimization of the many, the blows Jake LaMotta strikes against himself bind the champ with non-contenders who are taught the same falsehoods, endure parallel disillusionment, and subsequently manage (if lucky) to pull out a draw with their own impulses of suspicion and revenge. *We tried* is the message carried in the terror of those blows. *We believed and we tried. We fought to do it our way and lost everything. Go sing your fucking song elsewhere.*

2. America: Love It or Leave It.

A counterpart of Jake LaMotta's scream resounds in the voice of Bruce Springsteen. Throughout his career this performer's theme has been greaser life and frustration—how it goes for the young who disappear into Shop at grade nine or before and thereafter aren't in the picture.

Like LaMotta, greasers are teased and raddled by false

promises, media hype, the dream of unconditionedness. Unlike LaMotta, they're never awarded a minute's playing time in the great American upward-mobility match. Springsteen sings from the dead center of their sense both of possibility and of possibility frustrated. The longings (gonna win, gonna be Somebody) are vibrant; the singer's voice is full of cocky, choked, brazen-it-out anger—the anger of the unfashionable and unremediated and unknown, leaderless, lobbyless young on whom, as they cruise and booze, it's just now dawning, in the songs at least, that they've been sold out. Who's guilty? Teachers, testers, "guidance counselors," principals—The System. How exactly did it happen? They were suckered not by gatekeeper gamblers but by Shop, by Voc Ed, by legends of The Stars, by army commercials (Be All You Can Be), by Speed stores and stockcar flicks and ten thousand country and western "hits" about losers who win. . . .

The summit of talkback in Springsteen's music is the refrain of "Born in the USA" (1984). The song everywhere echoes (nowhere quotes) the bumper-sticker slogan conventionally understood, from above, as the epitome of working class jingoism—America: Love It or Leave It. Before the cut is finished, the refrain (the title itself) kicks powerfully against numbskull patriotism, conveying both class anger at betrayal and the longing to find a way back to love of country that's undefiled by exploitation.

The singer's assumed persona in the song is that of an unemployed Vietnam vet whose brother was killed at Khe San, and whose life is pure despair. ("End up like dog who's been beat too much/Till you spend half your life just covering up.") The song-story on its face centers on simple disillusionment. Romanticized, idealized America—the land of equals that the vet was taught to love—sent its working class

young men to fight a dirty war. And their exempted betters
—privileged protesters, choosers in the warm room—did dirt
on the soldiers who fought for them. Often contemptuous of
patriotism and oblivious of the class realities of the draft, they
forced working class high schoolers—few of the latter were
enthusiastic about the war—into the defensive jingoism of
the bumper sticker. And the result, as represented in "Born
in the USA," was a patriotism of the scream: love of country
after the fall, complicated and corrupted by the sense that
only through mindless braggadocio can America's America-
baiting, exploiting "educated classes" be repudiated.

Springsteen's actual scream near the song's end seems
an attempt to push toward yet more complex levels of feeling;
it's a patriotic outburst tortured with consciousness both of
its own vulnerability to exploitation, and of the death in the
USA of any ideal principle of unity and solidarity. *You call
us working stiff types*, says the talkback message. *You chuckle
at vulgar slobbish stupid macho jingos. But tell us this, draft
boards and recruiters and admen: who* made *the jingo? Who*
made *the patriot into the man of hate?*

3. We're All Equals Here.

Of necessity, talkback is a scrambler—accepting help from
any quarter however despised, convinced truth can fall from
the lips of a murderer, a self-torching crackhead, any so-called
deviant, not alone from elected officialdom, academicians,
and anchorpersons. What's more, talkback savors micro

details—sharply defined particulars casting light on attitudes and feelings otherwise obscure.

A telling example turns up in an early chapter of Norman Mailer's study of Gary Gilmore, *The Executioner's Song* (1979). The subject is what happens when workers know no better than to take seriously their employers' affirmations that we're all equals around here. The episode is shot through with grotesque humor, but because Gilmore's talkback to the myth of classlessness occurs almost on the eve of the brutal slaying that ultimately brings him before a state firing squad, there can be no smiles. The man is demented and violent— isn't to be seen as either ordinary or as innocent. But his experience nevertheless illuminates that of millions who, unlike him, learn early how to cope with the sentimental egalitarianism of the owning and employing classes—learn, that is, how to see through the sentimentality, how *not* to talk back.

Paroled in his early thirties from the maximum security prison in Illinois that was built to replace Alcatraz, Gilmore on the outside is bereft both of job experience and skills. He's been in and out of reform school and jail since age thirteen; in prison he was on Prolixin, by prescription, for long stretches; he has intelligence, an explosive temper, and familiarity with the arts of the survivor-con, but little knowledge of the ways of the work world. As a late entrant into that world, he resembles, in truth, a naïve stranger.

The small businessman (fifteen employees) who takes him on, Spencer McGrath, is a home and commercial insulator and garbage recycler, and a proudly democratic boss who tries never to pull rank—a decent man in the grip of a sponsored fantasy. At first Gilmore is puzzled and stiff, uncertain how to behave, trying to make an impression as a worker, but still a slave to the thieving habits of his past. Spencer learns that his new, ex-con employee is walking to work, and also that he's touchy about admitting he can't afford a car; believing "such pride was the makings of decent stuff," he offers to vouch for Gilmore to a used car dealer. Gilmore's standoffishness eases and Spencer is pleased: "[He] felt all right. It had taken a week but Gilmore appeared to be loosening up. He was coming to see that Spencer didn't like his people to think of him as a boss. He did the same work they did, and didn't want any superior relationship. If, as expected, his employees were faithful to what they were all trying to do, that was enough. No need to ride anybody."

Workers who at thirty have been coping with varieties of boss class behavior for a dozen years—coping with by-the-book foremen, with pinchers, with easy riders, with employers who actually think that their objectives are identical with those of their employees—have some feeling for the nature of the situation created by a superior who doesn't like "his people" to "think of him as a boss." They're clear about limits: how far one can go, how much boss bonhomie should be discounted, how much chaffing interaction is permissible, when one should (and shouldn't) close the distance, exactly which posture perfectly blends seemly deference and easygoing chumminess. Learning those limits is essential to working with and for imperial middle egalitarian fantasts who believe themselves to be living in a culture of classlessness.

But Gilmore the naïve stranger proves a slow learner. There's ineptitude on both sides, to be sure. Spencer McGrath, democratic nice guy, knows that Gilmore needs transportation, and knows that he'll need help paying for it. But his knowledge stops there. He doesn't know that Gilmore lacks a license, lacks car smarts to help him spot a lemon, lacks basic car repair know-how of the sort that can moderate discouragement at being saddled with a lemon. (Gilmore doesn't even know that jumper cables exist, much less how to use them.) In class terms Spencer is just far enough removed from his employee-equal to be unable to grasp how the parts of a loser's life work together against him: how the lemon that won't start in the morning lays a curse on the workday, how the surprise expenditure ($32 for a new battery) can shoot the budget, mock the hopeful plan for self-rehabilitation, sharpen the need for cheering hits of beer and weed.

Worse, Spencer doesn't realize that someone inexperienced at dealing with a no-boss boss will inevitably intrude on his boss's private space. Gilmore turns· up on a Sunday morning at Spencer's home after his car muffler falls off, convinced that his employer-pal would like to fix it. ("Gary didn't know to get it back by tightening the clamp."). After a fight with his girl, Gilmore calls on Spencer "between midnight and 2 A.M.," asking if Spencer and his wife "would like to play three-hand poker." He also drops in, drunk and uninvited, on Spencer's backyard barbecues, haranguing the guests about reincarnation.

Spencer finds some of this behavior "rude," but Gilmore, beguiled by his employer's buddy-buddy mien, isn't fazed. He seeks to entertain Spencer with prison stories about the time he stabbed a black fellow-con fifty-seven times (the anecdotes are followed by a request for a little afternoon time off). And when the employer who doesn't wish to be superior is at last driven to suggest that his employee change his ways, the employee stuns him with a patch of total candor, thereby convincing the employer that it's time for Gary Gilmore to go. The passage runs as follows:

" 'Gary,' Spence said, 'let's get down to something basic. Every week you're broke. Why don't you take the money you spend on beer and save it?' Gary said, 'I don't pay for beer.' 'Well, then, who in hell gives it to you?' Gary said, 'I just walk in a store, and take a six-pack.'

"Spence said, 'Nobody catches you, huh?' 'No.' 'How long you been doing that?' 'Weeks.' Spencer said, 'Steal a six-pack of beer every day and never been caught?' Gary said, 'Never.' Spencer said, 'I don't know. How come people get caught and you don't?' Gary said, 'I'm better than they are.' "

Listen, says the voice of talkback (in this instance, Gary Gilmore's voice), *I try to go straight, as straight as I can. I find a job and my boss says he's my pal, not my boss. I treat him the way pals should be treated. You take them your problems, right? You tell them the truth about yourself, right? You try to show them you're worth being friends with by boasting a little about your exploits, right? So what can I boast about but ripoffs and knifings? And he cuts me off. My pal says we're all equals and then he says go away, he thinks I'm "rude." He says I want you to change or I'll fire you . . . but really I'm your pal.*

In recent years a school of imperial middle business thought has been proposing love, not friendship, as the core of right relations between employers and employees. (The leader of the school is Tom Peters, author of *Passion for Excellence*, 1984.) An apogee of the influence of the myth of classless America, the business thought in question may eradicate, in time, for many employees, exact knowledge of the specifications of their situation: their dependency, the possibility of unceremonious severance, an overnight end to the pleasure of intimate fellowship with the lovingly democratic boss (as well as an end to paychecks). Even now the substance of that exact knowledge—its tangled contradictions—seems inexpressible except on the slant, in accounts of mistakes made by the lost, deviant, and condemned: the Gilmores of the world. Were it not for talkback, there might be *no* medium left in which the knowledge can still find its voice.

4. Whites, right! Blacks, get back!

At its most life-enhancing and energizing, talkback is funny. It extends an irresistible invitation to turn the hierarchy upside down, puncture personal pretensions, rejoice in the power of comic penetration to stir insurgencies against the tyranny of the bland. Few insurgencies have cut deeper into the hide of haughtiness, over the past two decades, than that led by Richard Pryor. And much of the power of this act derives from the variousness of the comedian's protest—his capacity to stage dramas of resistance at all levels of human life and on into the animal world as well. One Pryor turn, brilliantly mimetic, gives us the caged heaving anger of zoo creatures, monkeys and bears; another takes us inside a lion mooning Land-Rover eavesdroppers at feeding time on a Kenya wildlife reservation. Black preachers talk back to God, black fathers lay the law down to arrogant errant young ("get yo' ass home by 'leven"), black women challenge their would-be dominating men.

And white believers in themselves as necessarily superb are brought to life as characters whose mouths are filled with Grottlesex marbles—tidy, prissy, monotoned, unbending, soporific, rhythmless, *dumb* creatures whom nobody sane would wish to emulate.

"Pass the potatoes. Thank you, darling. Could I have a

bit of that sauce? How are the kids coming along with their studies? Think we'll be having sexual intercourse this evening? We won't? Well, what the heck."

There's more than this to the characterization, of course. Most tellingly, there's a recurring contrast between imperial middle ease and intimacy with authority, and black terror. An unctuous white pass-the-potatoes burgher greets a cop on the beat with confidently condescending affability: "Hel-lo, Officer Timson. Going bowling tonight?" Stopped for a speeding violation, asked for his license, Mr. Unctuous is all poise: "Yes, Officer, glad to be of help." A black similarly stopped trembles unto death, afraid to move. Indeed, he doesn't move without first spelling out descriptions of his movements in distinctly separated, slow-spoken words: "I-am-reaching-into-my-pocket-for-my-license-because-I-don't-want-to-be-a-mother-fucking-accident."

And the comedian probes the consequences of the terror, not alone its provenance. A black couple heads out for a night of dancing and Pryor asks, Why do they bother? They're taking dangerous chances out there on the road. A police car pulls the couple over. The cop's voice is fierce: "Put your hands up, take your pants down, spread your cheeks." Afterward, says Pryor, "You go home and beat your kids."

It's bitter laughter, obviously. The performer works inside the ironic slogans of his community (Whites, right! Blacks, get back!), drawing his audience close to the realities of an unending experience of humiliation. And everywhere the torrent of obscenities bespeaks the will to offend the true offenders, clean-spoken congratulators of the great American past and present. "We are here to celebrate two hundred years of white folks kicking ass. And my prayer is, How long will this bullshit go on?"

* * *

Talkback isn't "nice," to repeat. It lives by excess, not by the values reflected in such balanced, elegant concepts as that of double truth—personal and social responsibility. Its worst offenses, moreover, aren't against manners; often it sinks into race-baiting and Jew-baiting—viciousness even less pardonable than that at which its own protest is aimed. (A struggle for mind—for an end to the myth of classlessness— that seeks only to replace one mode of inhumanity with another is clearly not worth waging.) And in and of itself, talkback is powerless—no more capable of effecting a trans- formation of American political institutions than Ollie North, lone individualist, was capable of redirecting foreign policy. Neither equity nor salvation is attainable by sass, and the case is that there's not much sass: approximately a thou- sand audience-hours of *Cosby Show* platitude, say, for every quarter-hour of authentic talkback.

Yet at this hour talkback is what we have; best not to belittle it. It dares the imperial middle to achieve self- consciousness—to recognize the respects in which the mid- dle's automatic assurance of superiority of mind and morals is a species of fatuity. It dares the middle to understand that its enclosure in fantasy—its social confinement, its inability to see and value what is different from itself—amounts to a terrible impoverishment of being: of humor, passion, and truth. Talkback is *jazz*, the music of all nations dreaming (in the very late twentieth century) on freedom. It's the sound in which the whole world hears "the heartbeat of America" not as a commercial but as an exhortation to hope; time and again the beaten-down have found in its rhythms resources for revolt. The habit of dismissing it as crude and undiscip- lined is self-disabling; talkback is, in truth, the most precious capital that we possess.

• *Chapter 13* •

GROWINGPOINTS

*A*s this is written momentous events are in progress in Eastern Europe. Those who were entrapped behind the Iron Curtain, who were truly different from ourselves, permitted not a single expression of free thought, have risen up to choose our good. The temptation to read the events as justification for yet higher American levels of national self-satisfaction is obvious; no less obvious, one may hope, is the need to resist the temptation long enough for us to locate the parallels—limited but genuine— between our situation and that of the peoples now claiming their freedom.

Totalitarian socialism marched (according to its myth) in the vanguard of a world advance toward higher levels of fraternal selflessness than hitherto achieved. If it resorted to brutality, it did so because of the mean stubbornness of the forces of greed seeking to block the advance; if it silenced writers who charged it with moral self-deception and corruption, it did so because they were enemies of hope; if it shut off access to knowledge of competing systems, it did so because determined not to allow decadent distractions to slow progress toward justice. An immeasurably expensive, apparently invulnerable system of thought control

228 • THE IMPERIAL MIDDLE

and policing supported the myth, rendering challenge inconceivable.

And now, seemingly all at once, with an astounded and overjoyed world watching, the myth is overcome and whole nations launch themselves on the labor of inventing and sustaining democratic alternatives to the monstrous deceit that once bore them down.

A gulf separates the defeated myth from the myth with which this book has wrestled. Mass slaughter, forced labor, brainwashing are known to nobody born in this country; endless deadening shortages of food and housing are known to few; fear and inhibition do not stifle our critical impulse.

But this hardly legitimizes complacency and self-congratulation. Differences exist from culture to culture in the content of myths and in the forces marshaled in their support. But it doesn't follow that only when outright, state-initiated brutality is among those forces—only when freedom of thought and expression is at immediate risk—should the voice of protest ring loud. The myth of classlessness which thrives among us causes widescale injury and injustice. As we've seen, the work of critics who attempt to contend against it while observing the conventions and tones of academic discourse is highly susceptible to perversion—easily put to uses opposed to those originally intended. The metaphor of imprisonment with which the present book began ("a nation in shackles") can be criticized on the ground that the American example was a beacon lighting the Central European uprisings, and because real as opposed to metaphorical shackles haven't been felt in this country for longer than a century. But these are insufficient reasons for muting the attack on the myth of classlessness. The cause of freedom will prosper nowhere unless Americans resist the narcotizing "we won" state of mind and recognize their own need for a new awakening, new thinking, and a better proportioned sense of self.

Meeting that need is no simple project. The movement for change in this nation can't be galvanized, like movements abroad, by a single truth. As American critics of liberalism learned almost a half-century ago, our struggle against myth is inexpressible except in language dense in qualification; it involves learning how to hold opposed or competing values in immediate adjacency to each other with a view to mutual accommodation; it is necessarily a struggle on behalf of double truths.

The pivotal double truths can be quickly summarized. American faith in classlessness simultaneously whitewashes unearned advantages—and feeds the sense of possibility and energizes an invaluable, anti-determinist cast of mind. The American egalitarian spirit nourished by faith in classlessness is a major source of the improvisational spontaneity of our behavior and art—and is also a major wrecker of the idea of responsibility. (Where everyone who counts is held to be a striving imperial middler bent on personal betterment, those who regardless of class might hold themselves answerable for declines in aesthetic, intellectual, and moral standards hide out indifferently in the crowd.) And finally: defeating the myth of classlessness requires the amendment of public policy through scores of specific legislative and administrative actions—and requires as well profound changes in thought and feeling at levels utterly remote from that of public policy.

It is this subject—the revolution in sensibility—that bears strongest emphasis here at the end. My argument throughout has envisaged a political struggle to be waged in public forums. Federal, state, and municipal laws and regulations need to be re-examined with an eye to clarifying their class implications—the extent to which they ordain class advantages and disadvantages. Every area of public concern —the justice system, tax policy, health care, housing, job training, education, welfare—needs to be included in this re-examination. And there are leadership roles to be played, obviously, by ambitious officeholders and shrewd would-be candidates—men and women willing to stand on the side of significant change and capable of articulating political positions more immediately relevant to the whole electorate than any associated with yesteryear's liberalism. It's as yet unproven that vast popular support cannot be mustered for a drive to recover this nation's best self.

But accomplishing the political agenda will not in itself effect the necessary transformation; unprecedented events within private selves must accompany those taking place on the public stage. It's in the nature of things that these inner, hidden events will be infinitely various, differing with each individual's class and family situation, gender, occupation, religious faith, pattern of daily life. We are speaking of psychological transactions, small, often imperceptible shifts of perspective and attitude—brief awakenings of consciousness, impulses of correction, attempts at resisting stock response.

A man on a grocery checkout line watches an unhealthy-looking parent and child pay (partly with food stamps) for a basket of mainly non-nutritious items (Pepsi, candy, cigarettes, no fresh fruit, no veg). Disapproval, a basic class response, comes quickly but the man moves against it. His purpose isn't to deny the link between poor nutrition and degeneracy but to bring alive a class-banished truth: "The less money you have," as Orwell put it a half-century ago, "the less inclined you feel to spend it on wholesome food." The

man means to take a step forward from the moralizing response ("stupid improvident people"); his "new thinking" is
the kind that knows better than to bark at natives in bamboo
huts, that doesn't cut behavior off from its roots in social
reality, economic fact, settled, imperial middle arrangements
for the distribution of life-satisfactions and pleasures.

Once more: at a school Parents' Night a woman hears a
Hispanic father ask a serious but impossibly uninformed question about applying to college. Won't his son be "in trouble
with the authorities" if he applies to two places at one time?
Again the class response comes swiftly: surprise, vague amuse-
ment, condescension—but the woman tries to check it, playing over the question she's just heard in her mind. Because
new to the "application process," the man sees duplicity and
bad faith in it; she herself sees the same process as practically
a law of nature. ("It's just how the system works.") Kids
present themselves over and over ... get better at it ... learn
how to dope people out, to say things better, to sell themselves. Why would a father flinch at this?—Tonight: *Dear
Princeton, You alone I covet.* Tomorrow night: *Dear Brown,
You alone I covet....* But is the questioner a fool? Should his
qualm, naïve or not, be mine? What are the costs of institu-
tionalizing duplicity at an early age?

Small gestures, minuscule movements of mind. They
make nobody kinder and gentler, make nothing happen in
the public world. Ten million such gestures will not alter the
philosophy of social provision that must be transformed. But
ten million individual human efforts at comprehending that
others of different class have insides of their own will in time
matter—as growingpoints. Such efforts seed new mental
habits—that of interrupting the judgmental self by imagining
another mind's way of working, that of assuming (naturally,

comfortably) that minds different from one's own, regardless of their place in the hierarchy, have the capacity to teach.

"The longer I live, citizen," said Péguy, "the less I believe in the efficiency of an extraordinary sudden social revolution, improvised, marvelous, with or without guns and impersonal dictatorship, and the more I believe in the efficiency of modest, slow, molecular, definitive, social work." The effort to push past class vacuity is nothing if not modest, slow, and molecular, and is extremely demanding; it also ranks among the most rewarding kinds of "social work." As the habits of response that it fosters come into being, the mind edges its way inside the lie of classlessness, and glimpses the ideal which, by a paradox, can only be served if the lie is confronted and undone. That ideal is, of course, the original American vision of right democratic relationships among human beings. It is waiting now to be reclaimed; let us begin.

NOTES

Preface

9 obligations of genius: See, e.g., the novelist Paul Theroux's assertion, "My life is a paragon of noninvolvement," *People*, December 12, 1983, p. 124.

10 "divided by class": quoted in George Will, "A Case for Dukakis," *The Washington Post*, November 3, 1988, p. A27. Will called it "a national travesty that a presidential candidate denies class realities."

13 "without bias": Learned Hand, *The Spirit of Liberty* (New York: Knopf, 1952), p. 190.

Chapter 1: Talking About
Each Other

17 "get into class": quoted by Bernard Weinraub, "Dole Polishes His 'Poor Boy' Role Against 'Preppie' Bush," *The New York Times*, January 17, 1988, p. E5.

18 "Fred to Choate": Jules Feiffer, strip in *The Village Voice*, September 27, 1987, p. B2.

18 "eat a bowling ball": Ann Beattie, *Falling in Place* (New York: Random House, 1980), p. 88.

22 "salesmen and bartenders": *The New Yorker*, January 18, 1988, p. 92.

22 "nicer than hers": Hilda Dent, "From the Publisher," *Montgomery* (Ala.) *Magazine*, December 10–16, 1987, p. 2.

23 "how she *moves*": Michael Shnayerson, "Can Diane Sawyer Have It All?," *Vanity Fair*, September 1987, p. 140.

23 "no concrete goal": Gail Sheehy, "Why Gary Hart Destroyed Himself: Important New Evidence," *Vanity Fair*, September 1987, p. 188. I am indebted to Susan J. Douglas' acute commentary on class implications of the Sheehy and Shnayerson articles; see her "Blond Ambition," *In These Times*, October 28–November 3, 1987, pp. 12–13.

23 "Married . . . with Children": N. R. Kleinfeld, "Fox's Blue-Collar Comedy vs. ABC's: No Contest," *The New York Times*, December 1, 1988, p. B4.

24 "HAND-washing floors": "A Maid Is a Maid," *In These Times*, December 9–15, 1987, p. 4.

24 "has to do": This and the previous quotation in the paragraph are from "Hotel Bids Maids Hand-Scrub Floor," an AP dispatch in *The New York Times*, December 3, 1987, p. B15.

Chapter 2: Class Dismissed

30 "insignificant as you": Jilly Cooper, *Class* (New York: Knopf, 1981), pp. xvi–xvii.

30 "word than 'fuck' ": Cooper, p. 39. Ms. Cooper's views about the pervasiveness of class precisely match those of her countryman, George Orwell. In *The Road to Wigan Pier* (1937), Orwell writes: "The fact that has got to be faced is that to abolish class-distinctions means abolishing a part of yourself. Here am I, a typical member of the middle class. It is easy for me to say that I want to get rid of class-distinctions, but nearly everything I think and do is a result of class-distinctions. All my notions—notions of good and evil, of pleasant and unpleasant, of funny and serious, of ugly and beautiful—are essentially *middle-class* notions; my taste in books and food and clothes, my sense of honour, my table manners, my turns of speech, my accent, even the characteristic movements of my body, are the products of a special kind of upbringing and a special niche about half-way up the social hierarchy." (New York, Berkley ed., 1961, p. 137.)

31 "even in prole settings": Paul Fussell, *Class* (New York: Ballantine, 1983), p. 96.

32 "whole class racket": Fussell, pp. 213, 222–223.

32 dinner for four: Lewis Lapham, *Money and Class in America* (New York: Weidenfeld and Nicolson, 1988), p. 40.

32 fur bedspread: George Will, "Rodeo Drive, Street of Dreams," in *The Pursuit of Virtue and Other Tory Notions* (New York: Simon and Schuster, 1982), p. 351.

32 "her $24,995 dress": "Confessions of a Temp for Donald Trumpet," *Avenue*, February 1988, p. 154.

33 barns in his youth: Maureen Dowd, "Gore Lashes Out

at Rivals and Image," *The New York Times*, February 22, 1988, p. A12.

33 "Dole is one of us": Edmund Walsh, "Dole, Bush Duel Over Net Worth, Class Origins," *The Washington Post*, January 12, 1988, p. A1.

34 "breaking his pick": Peggy Noonan, *What I Saw at the Revolution* (New York: Random House, 1990), p.100.

36 class-based terminology: "In a period when work is seldom a calling and few of us find a sense of who we are in public participation as citizens, the lifestyle enclave, fragile and shallow though it often is, fulfills that function for us all." Robert N. Bellah, Richard Madsen, William M. Sullivan, Ann Swidler, and Steven M. Tipton, *Habits of the Heart* (New York: Harper & Row, 1985), p. 75.

36 "has value of its own": Anna Kisselgoff, "Stage: The Dancing Feet of Michael Jackson," *The New York Times*, March 6, 1988, p. 64.

37 "just means tasteless": Kim Hubbard and Anne Maier, "Pink Flamingos & Presleyana: The Strange Obsessions of Ole Miss Prof Charles Wilson," *People*, December 14, 1987, n. p.

38 applicant's SAT scores: This is current practice at Amherst College.

38 "where it all started": Dave Anderson, "Greek Loses an Out Bet," *The New York Times*, January 17, 1988, p. 17.

Chapter 3: The Imperial Middle

42 "homogeneous enterprise": Robert Wiebe, *The Opening of American Society* (New York: Knopf, 1985), p. 322.

42 "American society": Robert Bellah, et al., *Habits of the Heart*, p. 119. For an illuminating critique of professional sociologists who function as purveyors of the myth of class-lessness, see Barbara Ehrenreich, *Fear of Falling* (New York: Pantheon, 1989), pp. 18–19, 24–27.

45 "easily treated": *The New York Times*, January 3, 1988, p. 10.

45 New York subways: George Will, "The Politics of Sentimentality" and "Signs of Decay" in *The Pursuit of Virtue and Other Tory Notions* (New York: Simon and Schuster, 1982), pp. 224, 339.

45 shopping for it: See, e.g., Diana Ketcham, "Who Are We? Our Furniture Speaks Volumes," *The New York Times*, February 25, 1988, p. C1.

46 "fit into normal society": Susan Donna Fischer, *Harvard and Radcliffe Class of 1967 Twentieth Anniversary Report*, Cambridge, 1987, p. 262.

46 " 'shall be preserved' ": Stephen Lee Saltonstall, *Harvard and Radcliffe Twentieth Anniversary Report*, p. 174.

46 "aspects of our natures": *Harvard and Radcliffe Twentieth Anniversary Report*, p. 173.

48 "with Mrs. Rockefeller": Lapham, *Money and Class*, p. 174.

48 privileges associated therewith: "Harvard Chagrined by Agreement with Donors," *The New York Times*, November 15, 1987, p. 68. See also AP dispatch, "Harvard University

Trades Positions for Gifts," *Hampshire Gazette*, Northampton, Mass., November 15, 1987.

49 " 'smarter than me' ": Isabel Wilkerson, " 'Separate and Unequal': A View from the Bottom," *The New York Times*, March 1, 1988, p. A12.

Chapter 4: Appearance, Reality, Renunciation

57 "blue-collar look": Peter J. Boyer, *Who Killed CBS?* (New York: Random House, 1988), pp. 124–125.

58 "they actually are": Herbert Gans, *Deciding What's News* (New York: Vintage, 1980), p. 24. See also Professor Gans' "Bystanders as Opinion Makers: A Bottoms-Up Perspective," in *Gannett Center Journal* (Spring 1989), for a useful analysis of "top down [social] perspectives" in the media.

58 jackets and ties: Lewis Grizzard, *When My Love Returns from the Ladies Room, Will I Be Too Old to Care?* (New York: Villard, 1987), pp. 89, 169.

58 "over $50,000": E. J. Dionne, "Bush Still Ahead as End Nears but Dukakis Gains in Survey," *The New York Times*, November 6, 1958, pp. 1, 36.

59 "animus against gentility": James Harvey, *Romantic Comedy in Hollywood* (New York: Knopf, 1987), p. 248.

60 doctor and lawyer: The show, entitled "Call of the Wild," first aired in 1988.

62 in its depiction: On this and several related points,

see Mark Crispin Miller's shrewd study of sitcoms and commercials, "Deride and Conquer," in *Watching Television*, ed. Todd Gitlin (New York: Pantheon, 1986), pp. 206–213.

71 rich culture vultures: See, e.g., Twain's *The Innocents Abroad*, 1869 (New York edition, 1906).

Chapter 5: The Omni Syndrome

73 Trenton, New Jersey: price list courtesy of Sculpture Placement, Washington, D.C.

75 "corporate acquisition": Allen H. Neuharth, *INC.*, April 1989, p. 77.

76 "They embraced me": Lee Iacocca, *Iacocca* (New York: Bantam, 1984), p. 232.

76 "as they wish": Nelson Aldrich, *Old Money* (New York: Knopf, 1988), p. 93.

77 "being me": I borrow here from an unpublished paper by Laraine Einbinder produced for the Baruch College (CUNY) research seminar on "Class and Classlessness" that I taught in 1989. The Newhart segment, entitled "Malling in Love Again," first aired on May 8, 1989.

78 office is picketed: The episode, entitled "Curtains," aired in 1989.

80 "ski pole": *Harvard Alumni Gazette*, January 1989, p. 14.

80 "fix the truck": quoted by Maggie Murphy, "Loose Talk," *US: The Entertainment Magazine*, March 5, 1990, p. 8.

80 "the everything man": Tina Fredricks, catalog com-

mentary for Museum of Modern Art Andy Warhol show, 1989, quoted in *The New Republic*, March 27, 1989, p. 27.

81 "thought [it] was 'British' ": George Plimpton, *Paper Lion* (New York: Harper & Row, 1966), p. 55.

81 "higher than in baseball": *Paper Lion*, p. 124.

82 "the chateau towers": Plimpton, *Out of My League* (New York: Harper & Row, 1961), pp. 15, 17.

82 "to come into town": *Paper Lion*, p. 113.

83 "corner of the tongue": *Out of My League*, p. 71.

84 *"white man making black music"*: George W. S. Trow, *Within the Context of No Context* (Boston: Little, Brown, 1980), pp. 209–210.

85 "that could play it": The quotation, as well as the details of Ms. Franklin's life cited in this paragraph, are drawn from Peter Guralnick's brief, sensitive biography, "Aretha Arrives," in *Sweet Soul Music* (New York: Harper & Row, 1986), pp. 332–352.

85 "conjoint communicated experience": John Dewey, *Democracy and Education* (New York: Macmillan, 1916), p. 101.

86 "over there": "Bush sees kin as 'the little brown ones,' " *The Washington Post*, August 17, 1988, p. A22.

86 Bakker at lunch: Gary Wills, "Evangels of Abortion," *The New York Review of Books*, June 15, 1989, p. 21. For a survey of President Bush's tastes in sport, food, entertainment, and music, see Maureen Dowd, "For Bush, Culture Can Be a Sometime Thing," *The New York Times*, October 27, 1988, p. 1.

86 "snort you people": Quoted by Liza Grumwald in "Robin Williams Has a Big Premise!," Robin Williams interview, *Esquire*, June 1989, p. 120.

87 Cambridge intellectuals: "A Harvard Basher in Cam-

paign, Bush Now Is Backer," *The Wall Street Journal*, January 17, 1989, p. 1.

87 New Haven days: "Bush Recalls the Play," *The New York Times*, June 6, 1988, p. C7.

87 "macho man": quoted in "Capital Line," *USA Today*, February 8, 1990, p. 4A.

88 "see it again": Anne-Marie Schiro, "Following a Tough Act with Impeccable Taste," *The New York Times*, January 21, 1989, p. 8.

88 "George comes up with": "White House Gala à la Barbara Bush: Changes Are Subtle," *The New York Times*, June 28, 1989, p. C12.

90 "I have lived": Ralph Waldo Emerson, "The American Scholar," *Essays and Lectures* (New York: Library of America, 1983), p. 60.

92 "warm place to shit": Earl Butz, quoted in *Political Profiles: The Nixon/Ford Years* (New York: Facts on File, 1979), p. 104.

92 "that's high living": quoted in "Parks at the Pierre," *Eye*, May 15–22, 1989, p. 10.

Chapter 6: Class Coverup: Three Masking Languages

96 "sell her child?": The question was posed in exactly these terms by Barbara Ehrenreich, in "The Lesson of Mary Beth," *New York Post Books*, March 5, 1989, a review of *A Mother's Story* by Mary Beth Whitehead with Loretta Schwartz-Nobel

(New York: St. Martin's, 1989). My account of Ms. White-head's motivations owes much to Ms. Ehrenreich's thoughtful analysis of the Whitehead–Schwartz-Nobel book.

96 "manipulative and exploitative": Robert Hanley, "Three Experts Say Baby M's Mother Is Unstable," *The New York Times*, February 11, 1987, p. B4.

96 "not a surrogate mother": *A Mother's Story*, p. 136.

97 "are terminated": See transcript of Judge Harvey Sorkow's decision in *The New York Times*, April 4, 1987, p. B2.

97 "for the pediatrician": *A Mother's Story*, p. 160.

100 "their own genetic child": Quotations in this and the following paragraph are from *A Mother's Story*, pp. 8, 11, 12, 68.

102 "things went awry": quoted by Geoffrey Stokes, "Press Clips," *The Village Voice*, August 2, 1988, p. 8. It was Mr. Stokes' justifiably angry response ("Wh-a-a-t? Who is [Cronkite] talking about? Roosevelt? Stalin? Mao? *Hitler?*") that alerted me to the class implications of the Rather-Cronkite exchange.

107 "is not the news": All quotations in this and the succeeding paragraph are from Mark A. Uhlig, "Breaking Through a Murderous Silence," *The New York Times*, November 15, 1987, p. E9.

108 "striking out": David L. Bazelon, *Questioning Authority: Justice and Criminal Law* (New York: Knopf, 1988), p. 94.

109 "guys named José": Erica Manfred, "On Leaving Civilization," *The Village Voice*, March 29, 1988.

Chapter 7: Daily Discourses

112 "threat and control": *The New York Times*, December 24, 1989, p. 1. All quotations in the following six paragraphs are from this "special report."

116 "antics of her kids": Walter Goodman, "Roseanne Is No Cousin to Archie Bunker," *The New York Times*, January 1, 1989, p. H29. For a wholly different and trenchant perspective on Roseanne Barr, see Barbara Ehrenreich, "The Wretched of the Hearth," *The New Republic*, April 2, 1990, pp. 28–31.

117 "the way to college": Fred Hechinger, *The New York Times*, October 26, 1988, p. B11. Quotations in the following paragraph are also from this piece.

118 *"good, safe school"*: Dirk Johnson ' ᵃ City's Unwelcome Lesson About Schools and Class," *The New York Times*, April 2, 1989, p. E5.

119 "YOUR BROKER": Tim Stone, "Making Nice to Your Stockbroker," *The New York Times*, August 27, 1989, Section 3, p. 10.

120 "Lillywhites of London": Patricia Leigh Brown, "When the Sport Shapes the House and Grounds," *The New York Times*, August 17, 1989, p. C1.

120 "gown is de rigueur": Anne-Marie Schiro, "Looks That Will Sparkle for Holiday Parties," *The New York Times*, October 15, 1989, p. 58.

121 "going to learn anyhow": Don Wycliff, "Still Shunning the Black Doll," *The New York Times*, September 4, 1989, p. 26.

121 "open to the public": "Plutocrats and Moralizers," *The New York Times*, August 22, 1989, p. A22.

122 "society failed them?": Isabel Sawhill, "Exact Words," *The New York Times*, July 25, 1989, p. A20.

122 "imagine poverty": Charles Péguy, *Basic Verities* (New York: Pantheon, 1943), p. 119.

Chapter 8: School: The Fairness Zone

129 "universally valid ones": Karl Marx and Friedrich Engels, *The German Ideology* (London: Lawrence and Wishart, 1974), pp. 65–66.

132 failed in Camden: See Joseph F. Sullivan, "Judge Finds School Finance System in Jersey Is Constitutionally Flawed," *The New York Times*, August 26, 1988, p. 7.

135 "happier than I am": William H. McGuffey, *McGuffey's Newly Revised Eclectic Second Reader* (Cincinnati, 1843), pp. 47–50.

135 "with equal precision": William T. Harris, quoted by David Tyack, *The One Best System: A History of American Urban Education* (Cambridge: Harvard University Press, 1974), p. 61.

136 producing strikebreakers: See Ira Katznelson and Margaret Weir, "Training for the Workplace," Chapter 6, in *Schooling for All* (New York: Basic Books, 1985), pp. 150–177; the discussion of institutes and strikebreaking appears on pp. 167–168.

136 "lower industrial class": quoted by Joel Spring in *The American School, 1642–1985* (New York: Longman, 1986), p. 265.

139 midwestern high school: August B. Hollingshead,

Elmtown's Youth (New York: J. Wiley, 1949). See especially Chapter 8 "The High School in Action," p. 163ff.

140 more per year: See Natalie Rogoff, "Local Social Structure and Educational Selection," in *Education, Economy, and Society*, ed. A. H. Halsey et al. (New York: Free Press of Glencoe, 1961), p. 246; John C. Flanagan, *Project Talent: The American High School Student* (Pittsburgh: University of Pittsburgh, 1964), and John C. Flanagan and William C. Cooley, *Project Talent: One Year Follow-up Studies* (Pittsburgh: University of Pittsburgh, 1966), p. 96; William H. Sewell and Robert M. Hauser, "Causes and Consequences of Higher Education Models of the Status Attainment Process," *American Journal of Agricultural Economics*, December 1972, p. 851ff.; U.S. Bureau of Census, *Current Population Reports*, Series P-20, No. 241, "Social and Economic Characteristics of Students," 1972. Still the best overview of schooling in relation to class differentials is that provided by Daniel Rossides, *The American Class System* (Boston: Houghton Mifflin, 1976), Part II, Chapter 6, "Class and Differentials in the Educational Careers of Children," p. 200ff. My assertions concerning family income and aid packages are based on private conversations with financial aid officers.

140 standard of evaluation: see Howard S. Becker, "Social Class Variations in the Teacher-Pupil Relationship," in Robert R. Bell and Holger R. Stub, eds., *The Sociology of Education: A Sourcebook* (Homewood, Ill.: Dorsey Press, 1968), p. 155ff. See also Ray C. Rist, "Student Social Class and Teacher Expectations: The Self-Fulfilling Prophecy in Ghetto Education," *Harvard Educational Review*, August 1970, p. 411ff.

141 similar charges: The most effective recent indictment is found in Samuel Bowles and Herbert Gintis, *Schooling in Capitalist America* (New York: Basic Books, 1976).

143 "help to provide": George S. Counts, *The Selective*

Character of American Secondary Education (Chicago, Chicago University Press, 1922), pp. 151–152.

143 "do some good": W. Lloyd Warner, Robert J. Havighurst, and Morton B. Loeb, *Who Shall Be Educated?* (New York: Harper and Bros., 1944), p. 95.

143 academic analyses: Even as strongly argued a work as Diane Ravitch's *The Great School Wars: New York City, 1805–1973* (New York: Basic Books) repeatedly turns away from class issues, assigning primary importance to "value clashes among discordant ethnic, cultural, racial, and religious groups" (p. 404).

145 "fourth grade": E. D. Hirsch, "A Postscript," *Change*, July–August 1988, p. 26.

146 blame themselves: See Robert Lane, *Political Ideology* (New York: Free Press of Glencoe, 1962), pp. 68–71.

Chapter 9: History: The Fate of Autonomy

149 "slopshop entrepreneurs": Sean Wilentz, *Chants Democratic: New York City & the Rise of the American Working Class, 1788–1850* (New York: Oxford University Press, 1984), pp. 120, 145.

151 "not crush them": Bernard Bailyn, *Ideological Origins of the American Revolution* (Cambridge, Mass.: Harvard University Press, 1967), p. 319.

151 " 'cases be obeyed' ": The pamphlets cited in this paragraph are quoted in Bailyn, pp. 307–308.

152 "falls on his feet": Ralph Waldo Emerson, "Self-Reliance," in *Essays and Lectures* (New York: Library of America, 1983), p. 275.

153 "social improvement": Herbert Gutman, "The Reality of the Rags-to-Riches Myth," in Stephan Thernstrom and Richard Sennett, eds., *Nineteenth Century Cities: Essays in the New Urban History* (New Haven: Yale University Press, 1968), p. 122.

153 "security and dignity": Stephan Thernstrom, *Poverty and Progress: Social Mobility in a Nineteenth Century City* (Cambridge: Harvard University Press, 1964), p. 164.

153 ambitious and industrious: A succinct discussion of "Social Mobility in America," with emphasis on the late twentieth century, appeared in *The Wilson Quarterly*, Winter 1987, pp. 93–139. Using Census Bureau figures and reporting income dynamics over two generations, the *Quarterly* divided the population into income quintiles; it found much movement within the middle income sectors (the second, third, and fourth quintiles), little movement between the top and bottom quintiles. (Two percent of those in the highest income quintile had parents who were in the bottom quintile; 9 percent of those in the lowest quintile had parents in the highest quintile.) The most perceptive analysis of current statistics on "middle class" incomes is Stephen Rose's commentary on *The American Profile Poster* (New York: Pantheon, 1986). Rose notes that "the top 2% of the holders of wealth control over one-half of all financial assets," and argues that partly for this reason "very few people in households in the $15,000–100,000 range feel that they wield economic clout" (p. 33).

157 "in the world": Phillip Taft and Philip Ross, "American Labor Violence: Its Causes, Character, and Outcome," in

The History of Violence in America, Hugh Davis Graham and Ted Robert Gurr, eds. (New York: Praeger, 1969), p. 281.

157 corporate liberalism: See James Weinstein, *The Corporate Ideal in the Liberal State: 1900–1918* (Boston: Beacon Press, 1968), especially Chapters I–III.

163 "hold and lift": Elbert Hubbard, *A Message to Garcia* (East Aurora, N.Y.: The Roycrofters, 1899), pp. 4–5.

165 "made the money": *Iacocca*, p. 128.

167 to transform it: See Harvard Sitkoff, *The Struggle for Black Equality, 1954–1980* (New York: Hill and Wang, 1981), Chapter 2, pp. 41–68.

Chapter 10: Public Policy in the Classless State

175 escaped military service: See Lawrence M. Baskir and William K. Straus, *Chance and Circumstance: The Draft, the War and the Vietnam Generation* (New York: Vintage, 1978), p. 5. The other draft offender and deferment statistics in the paragraph are from this work, as are the materials in the following two paragraphs concerning unofficial studies of draft inequities (see Baskir and Straus, pp. 6–10).

177 "cattle off to slaughter": James Fallows, "What Did You Do in the Class War, Daddy?" *Washington Monthly*, October 1975. All quotations in this paragraph are from the Fallows article.

177 "with 100% certainty": quoted in Baskir and Straus, p. 39. Data and quotations in this and the next paragraph are from the same work, pp. 47–50.

179 "told to do": John O'Sullivan and Alan M. Meckler, *The Draft and Its Enemies* (Urbana, Ill.: Illinois University Press, 1974), p. 243.

179 "approximately the same": Baskir and Straus, p. 16.

180 "loss of deferment": The quotations in this and the two preceding paragraphs are from O'Sullivan and Meckler, p. 242.

181 "educationally disadvantaged": Rev. Theodore M. Hesburgh, in Baskir and Straus, pp. xi–xii.

184 "community-minded and selfish": Ellen Carol Du-Bois, "Working Women, Class Relations, and Suffrage Militance: Harriet Stanton Blatch and the New York Woman Suffrage Movement, 1894–1909," *The Journal of American History*, June 1987, p. 38.

184 "neediest Americans": Ann Shola Orloff, "The Political Origins," in Theda Skocpol, Margaret Weir, et al., eds., *The Politics of Social Policy in the United States* (Princeton, N.J.: Princeton University Press, 1985), pp. 47–48.

184 "deserving poor people": Theda Skocpol, "The Limits of the New Deal System and the Roots of Contemporary Welfare Dilemmas," in *The Politics of Social Policy*, p. 296. For an extended treatment of the same theme in the last two decades, see Michael Katz's invaluable *The Undeserving Poor* (New York, 1990), especially Chapters 4 and 5 ("Interpretations of Poverty in the Postindustrial City" and "The Underclass?").

185 ("however unpleasant"): Edward C. Banfield, *The Unheavenly City* (Boston: Little, Brown, 1970), p. vii.

185 "class culture": Banfield, pp. 53–54.

187 "savings and loan associations": Reeve Vanneman and Lynn Weber Cannon, *The American Perception of Class* (Philadelphia: Temple University Press, 1987), p. 304.

188 "cause poverty": Sidney Blumenthal, *The Rise of the*

Counter-Establishment (New York: Times Books, 1986), p. 293.

188 and the poor: Charles Murray, *Losing Ground* (New York: Basic Books, 1984), pp. 31, 33.

Chapter 11: Classlessness and the Struggle for Mind

194 "strong and sure": Michael Gold, "Towards Proletarian Art," in *The Liberator*, February 1921, quoted in Daniel Aaron, *Writers on the Left* (New York: Harcourt Brace and World, 1961), p. 88.

197 "have been lost": Richard Hofstadter, *The Age of Reform* (New York: Knopf, 1955), p. 5. The Hofstadter quotations in this and the next two paragraphs are found on pp. 59, 18, 185, 197, 205, 210.

199 "in the family": Robert Merton, *Social Theory and Social Structure* (Glencoe, Ill.: Free Press, 1949), p. 152. The quotations from *Social Theory* that follow in this and the next two paragraphs are found on pp. 131, 139, 146, 147, 147, 153, and 427.

205 "morally implacable": Stanley Elkins, *Slavery* (Chicago: Chicago University Press, 1959), p. 161. Subsequent quotations from *Slavery* in this and the following paragraphs are found on pp. 84 and 198–199.

208 "moral agonizing": Charles Murray, *Losing Ground* (New York: Basic Books, 1984), p. 33. Other quotations from *Losing Ground* in this and the next paragraph are found on pp. 31, 33, and 227–228.

208 "by choice": Ronald Reagan, quoted in *The New York Times*, March 22, 1981, p. 30.

208 "paying for it": Edwin Meese, quoted in *The New York Times*, February 19, 1986, p. A18.

208 "passion of compassion": Irving Kristol, "Skepticism, Meliorism, and *The Public Interest*," in *The Public Interest*, Fall 1985, p. 38.

Chapter 12: American Talkback

214 "*not a cockroach*": Stephen Bach, *Final Cut* (New York: Morrow, 1985), p. 166. Subsequent quotations from this work in the next five paragraphs are found on pp. 164–166.

219 be repudiated: My analysis borrows from Benj DeMott, "The Future Is Unwritten: Working Class Youth Culture in England and America," *Critical Texts*, Vol. 5, 1, 1988. The author is my son.

221 "decent stuff": Norman Mailer, *Executioner's Song* (New York: Warner, 1980), p. 71. Subsequent quotations from the work in this and succeeding paragraphs are found on pp. 72 and 151–153.

223 employers and employees: I discuss this proposal at length in "Threats and Whimpers: The New Business Heroes," *New York Times Book Review*, October 26, 1986, Sec. 7, p. 1.

224 "home by 'leven": Richard Pryor, *That Nigger's Crazy*, 1974. Quotations from Pryor in the next four paragraphs are also from this album.

225 "bullshit go on?": Richard Pryor, *Bicentennial Nigger*, 1976.

Chapter 13: Growingpoints

230 "wholesome food": George Orwell, *The Road to Wigan Pier* (New York: Berkley, 1961), p. 88.

232 "social work": Charles Péguy, *Basic Verities*, tr. Ann and Julian Green (New York: Pantheon, 1943), p. 119.

ACKNOWLEDGMENTS

Late in 1981 my daughter Jo and her partner, Jeff Kreines, documentary filmmakers, finished two years of work on a film called *Seventeen*, a two-hour feature on working class youngsters in a Muncie, Indiana, high school. The film was to attain very high rank among American documentaries. It's described by Vincent Canby of *The New York Times* as "ferociously provocative, one of the best reports on American life to be seen on a theater screen." It's shown and lavishly praised all round the world—London, Paris, Toronto, Brisbane, etc. In a minute I'll be quoting some of the notices, not solely out of father's pride.

But the notices in question came a good while after the film was made. The backers of the project were Xerox, the National Endowment for the Humanities, and PBS; when they saw bits of the movie, which they had contracted to show nationally on public TV, they tried to suppress it and succeeded.

It wasn't *my* movie, wasn't my problem; my daughter was in her thirties and had been a professional in her field for nearly ten years. No matter. For many months I had the big imposing voices of the Imperial Middle in my ears—the head of PBS, the head of Xerox, the TV critic of the *Times*, a crew of self-appointed custodians of the American Good and True. I heard those voices speaking unfairly and abusively of my own daughter, charging her with misrepresentation, unethical behavior and worse. A succession of false accusations, sanctimoniously phrased. William F. Buckley claimed (in the *Washington Post*) that Jo "trapped blotto teenagers into talking about other teenagers they have seduced." The *Christian Science Monitor* said she "induced" youngsters to reveal "the worst side of their character." The *Nation* weighed in with innuendoes, complaining that a "big city filmmaker" was exploiting unwary smalltowners. (My daughter's home—now and for most of the past twenty years—is a small town in Alabama.) PBS's Larry Grossman, speaking for white gentility everywhere, called her film "ghastly."

For a year and more it looked as though establishmentarian bullies would actually manage to kill the movie. Jo is a tough kid—"kid"? let it go: kids stay young to their parents, who feel their vulnerability to the very end—but these people knew how to hurt.

What caused the trouble? The high school pupils in the movie swore a lot and smoked dope on film. They talked about fondling and screwing. Astonishing. They weren't sweet to their teachers. They got along extremely well with people of other races (I am talking about blacks and whites "going together"), since everybody shared an intelligently critical view of the godly preceptors who condescended to them. They often beer-partied with their own parents. The movie was held together by a central figure—a wonderfully animated, bright, plucky, teenaged girl. She swore, smoked, defied fools in authority, all of it. The forces of the Good and True looked at her, looked at the blacks, looked at the "Shedown" parents—"Shedtown" is what Muncie calls its working class section—and were revolted. Because they lacked knowledge of American working class life—understood neither the causes of the objectionable behavior nor the reasons some of it laid a claim to respect—they had to hang the messenger: had to call my daughter a liar. And the excruciation of this was that the movie remains for me the truest and most loving account of working class life anybody in this country has yet produced. And I am not alone:

"You have to reach back to François Truffaut's *The 400 Blows* to recall a similarly searing matter-of-factness about the anarchy of school and the yawning gap between teenagers and adults. *Seventeen* tingles with the urgency of headlines not yet written, as it catches kids on the run from nothingness. Remarkable."

—Jay Carr, *The Boston Globe*

"Nothing like it has ever been recorded on film before, in so much sympathetic detail. This is one of the least fraudulent and condescending films about adolescence ever made."

—David Chute, Los Angeles *Herald Examiner*

"A must-see. *Seventeen* is a poignant, deeply affecting portrait of working class teenagers."

—Sheila Benson, *Los Angeles Times*

"Standing far apart from—and above—the more or less fabricated visions of teenage angst or teenage achievement ... It's *Seventeen* that haunts the memory. It has the characters and the language—as well as the vitality and honesty—that are the raw material of the best fiction."

—Vincent Canby, *The New York Times*

"I wasn't able to watch another foot of film for days, because *any* movie pales after seeing *Seventeen*. The single most important American documentary I've ever seen."

—Michael Ventura, *Los Angeles Weekly*

"It is not for technique alone that *Birth of a Nation* is so highly regarded, but for the giddy delight produced by the spectacle of racist hatred, unbridled and unashamed. DeMott and Kreines produce its opposite, in a film that calmly and simply contemplates the reality of an integrated educational system—that the races of their own accord can come together and relate freely and honestly *and* sexually. It is not an easy vision for America to deal with in this particular space and time. But the force of the truths that DeMott and Kreines bring forth cannot be ignored. They constitute a true *voyage à travers l'impossible* that America must make if its soul can ever hope to heal itself."

—David Ehrenstein, *Film: The Frontline 1984*, Arden Press

"Searingly candid, powerful, refreshing. One can discern underneath the bravado, hostility, rebelliousness, and barrage of profanity a code of morality that could flourish if given half a chance. *Seventeen* performs a valuable service by its honesty."

—William Wolf, Gannett News Service

"DeMott and Kreines lived in Muncie for almost two years. Working without hidden cameras or even telephoto lenses, [they] kept within a few feet of their subjects, DeMott concentrating on the girls and Kreines on the boys, their fast film stock and one-person rigs eliminating the need for crew or lights. DeMott and Kreines' method allowed them the luxury of watching events develop; one of the ironies of *Seventeen* being cut from Middletown was that DeMott and Kreines were far closer than any of their colleagues to the Lynds' participant-observer techniques. The DeMott-Kreines style has an extraordinary intimacy.... More than most documentaries, *Seventeen* performs the useful function of showing what part of our reality we regard as truly scandalous.... The fear of presenting an interracial couple on TV is a greater scandal than any romance could be."

—J. Hoberman, *The Village Voice*

"Here is a film they truly didn't want you to see, 'they' being two of the co-sponsors, the Xerox corporation and the Public Broadcasting System.... The basic problem with *Seventeen* was that the film's sponsors sent the filmmakers out to make a film that told the truth and promoted a positive, upper-middle-class image. Instead, Jo DeMott and Jeff Kreines came back with a film that showed what they saw.

"Muncie had been the subject of a controversial sociological study published in 1929, sponsored by John D. Rockefeller. That study had come back with results totally opposed to those for which Rockefeller had hoped.... Rockefeller wanted a study showing there was no class system in the middle-sized community. The study proved there was a rigid class system. History repeated itself with DeMott and Kreines.... Nothing in the film is simple; no good guys and bad guys. This film is undoubtedly the way it was. It is a dense, disturbing look at a section of America and America's future. When Xerox and PBS saw it, they refused to air it. Now that it can be seen, it should be. A dramatic, compelling film."

—Ted Mahar, Portland *Oregonian*

"Intriguing, revealing, candid, sympathetic—nothing in the pic rings untrue."

—*Variety*

"A powerful swarm of intimate, sometimes shocking images from the lives of working-class teenagers for whom class will be destiny."

—Sherryl Connelly, New York *Daily News*

"A film of rare beauty."

—*Liberation*, Paris

Let me finish. The forces of light—the Imperial Middle —hated the movie, hated Jo. They tried to take the movie away from her—aimed to prevent Jo and Jeff from hanging on to their right to show it on their own. They put the knock on both filmmakers unrelentingly, leaking extremely harsh stuff to the media. People of power absolutely determined that their corporation, their medium, their federal agency not be associated with "offensive" truth. All because, for two hours, a movie spoke truth. *Seventeen* evoked a whole malfunctioning social order: bad schools, pointless jobs, self-deceiving authority, social classes that never saw a level playing field. And the movie was clearly if unsentimentally on the side of the smart, vibrant, coarse-spoken, decent-hearted, systematically fucked-over working class youngsters whose stories it told. Lives weren't marginalized as in decorously solicitous "specials" on the homeless, the poor, the minorities. They were seen instead as enmeshed in a self-deluding, middle-American class society lost in dogmas of classlessness—a society whose untruthfulness has destructive impact all across the social spectrum.

Who could face this? Solution: suppress the movie.

I lived the experience as though it was coming at *me*. They—Jo DeMott and Jeff Kreines—lived it as reality.

I had a tiny reputation as an essayist—but it was no good. No *use*. There was no way I could tell the story without appearing to puff my own young. Frustration. I got over it, naturally. In your sixties you get over things. Rage gave way to thinking. I worked at grasping what the basic problem was, *why* people of the Good and True PBS stripe couldn't stand reality and had to consign the rest of us to one hundred years of Mahsterpiece Theatre tranquilizers. I cooled it. After a bitter, frustrating, expensive struggle, Jo and Jeff won control of *Seventeen*. The movie got shown—in theaters. (Public TV and the NEH have never let the filmmakers within a mile of another grant and no doubt never will.) The movie got shown and its extraordinary quality got recognized.

And I got educated, that's the only phrase for it. I woke up. I saw that the class problem went way beyond the movie, touched the darkest, deepest strains of American life. I tried to find an approach—impersonal to a degree but not drying up anger—that would enable me to speak to the problem. In time I stopped being a father defending his grownup kid and pushed myself to see things in the round. My daughter —all four of my children (two sons and two daughters, each living a life that reaches beyond the limits of the imperial middle world of their birth and rearing)—helped me. I don't know whether I've got it right, but I do know that, with this piece of writing, maybe for the first time ever, *they* knew where I was coming from. The book is dedicated of course to my daughter Jo. But it's one of those situations in which dedications don't touch the facts either of feeling or knowledge. What Joey taught me *is* this book.

* * *

Peggy DeMott, my wife, read the work critically, draft by draft; her suggestions were invaluable. Equally invaluable were two, extended, written commentaries on Chapter IX, "History: The Fate of Autonomy," by Benj DeMott, my younger son; I borrow his ideas and insights here and elsewhere, usually without explicit acknowledgement, but any errors are my own. Alan D. Williams was the first to confirm my hope that the book I wanted to write would find a publisher. My editor, Connie Roosevelt, gave me what every writer covets: straight, intelligent, unselfprotective responses each step of the way. For generous help of many kinds, special thanks to Donald Bigelow, Willis Bridegam, Henry Ferris, W. Gregory Gallagher, Margaret Groesbeck, David Jackson, Michael Kasper, Jeff Kreines, Gerard McCauley, Amy Meeker, James Merrill, Floyd Merritt, Richard Todd, and Phyllis Westberg.

INDEX

Pappas, Ike, 57
Parton, Dolly, 70
Péguy, Charles, 122, 232
Penny, Gerald, 13
People, 36, 37
Perales, Cesar A., 106–107
Peters, Tom, 223
Pinkertons, 156
Plimpton, George, 81–83, 88–89
Podhoretz, Norman, 202–205, 207
Poe, Edgar Allan, 142
Price, George, 17
Pryor, Richard, 224–225
Public Interest, The, 122, 208

Rainier, prince of Monaco, 37
Rather, Dan, 102
Reagan, Nancy, 76, 80
Reagan, Ronald, 76, 158, 182, 208
Rice, Donna, 23
Rockefeller, David, 47, 48
Ross, Phillip, 156
Rowan, Andrew S., 163

St. John, Christopher, 46
Salk, Lee, 92
SATs, 38, 39
Sawhill, Isabel, 122
Sawyer, Diane, 23, 26
Scorsese, Martin, 213, 214
Selective Service, 179–180
Sevareid, Eric, 102–103
Sinatra, Frank, 148
Skocpol, Theda, 184
Sports Illustrated, 81
Springsteen, Bruce, 218–219
Stahl, Leslie, 108
Steinberg, Lisa, 106, 119
Stern, Betsy, 100–101
Stern, William, 100–101

Taft, Phillip, 156
Television Programs:
　Public Affairs:
　　Face the Nation, 108
　　60 Minutes, 81
　Police Shows:
　　Cagney and Lacey, 66–70, 71
　　Hill Street Blues, 71

Sitcoms:
　All in the Family, 72, 76, 115
　Beverly Hillbillies, 72
　Bob Newhart Show, 76–77
　Cheers, 71
　The Cosby Show, 52, 60–64, 226
　Designing Women, 77–79
　Diff'rent Strokes, 76
　The Honeymooners, 115
　Married... with Children, 23
　Roseanne, 115
　Sanford and Son, 72
Serial drama:
　L.A. Law, 70
　thirtysomething, 71
　M'A'S'H, 70
Variety shows:
　Hee Haw, 86
　Laugh-in, 76
　Late Night with David Letterman,
　　19, 20, 25
Tiffany, 23
Touré, Sekou, 47
Tremain, Alan, 24, 25
Trilling, Lionel, 193–197, 199, 202,
　207, 208, 209
Trump, Donald, 47, 66
Twain, Mark, 71

Uhlig, Mark, 106–107

Vanity Fair, 23, 25
Vietnam War, 175–181, 190, 218
Village Voice, The, 80, 109

Wall Street Journal, The, 24
War on Poverty, 182
Warhol, Andy, 80
Weaver, Sigourney, 91
Webster, Noah, 152
Weed, Thurlow, 158
Wexler, Jerry, 83, 85
Whitehead, Mary Beth, 96–101
Whitman, Walt, 34
Wiebe, Robert, 42
Wilberforce, William, 206
Wilentz, Sean, 150
Will, George, 32